THE CREATION OF THE
CONSTITUTION

New Essays on American Constitutional History

Other Titles in this Series:

THE CREATION OF THE CONSTITUTION

by Max M. Edling

Published by the
American Historical Association
400 A Street, SE
Washington, DC 20003
www.historians.org

and sponsored by the
Institute for Constitutional History
at the New-York Historical Society
and the George Washington University Law School

ABOUT THE AUTHOR

MAX M. EDLING is a member of the History Department of King's College London and a historian of the American founding and the early federal government. He is the author of *A Revolution in Favor of Government: Origins of the U.S. Constitution and the Making of the American State* and *A Hercules in the Cradle: War, Money, and the American State 1783-1867.*

The New Essays on American Constitutional History series is also sponsored by the Institute for Constitutional History at the New-York Historical Society and the George Washington University Law School.

© 2018 by the American Historical Association
ISBN: 978-0-87229-211-6

An earlier version of this essay was published as "A More Perfect Union: The Framing and Ratification of the Constitution," in *The Oxford Handbook of the American Revolution*, ed. Edward G. Gray and Jane Kamensky (New York: Oxford University Press, 2013), 388-406. Reproduced by permission of Oxford University Press (http://global.oup.com/academic).

Published in 2018 by the American Historical Association. As publisher, the American Historical Association does not adopt official views on any field of history and does not necessarily agree or disagree with the views expressed in this book.

Library of Congress Cataloging-in-Publication Data

Names: Edling, Max M., author.
Title: The creation of the Constitution / by Max M. Edling.
Description: Washington, DC : American Historical Association, 2018. | Series: New essays on American constitutional history | "Sponsored by the Institute for Constitutional History at the New-York Historical Society and the George Washington University Law School." | Includes bibliographical references.
Identifiers: LCCN 2018038008 | ISBN 9780872292116 (paperback)
Subjects: LCSH: Constitutional history--United States--18th century. | United States--Politics and government--1783-1789.
Classification: LCC KF4541 .E279 2018 | DDC 342.7302/9--dc23
LC record available at https://lccn.loc.gov/2018038008

TABLE OF CONTENTS

Series Introduction

N ew Essays on American Constitutional History is published by the American Historical Association, in association with the Institute for Constitutional Studies. This series follows the lead of its predecessor, the Bicentennial Essays on the Constitution, published by the AHA under the editorship of Herman Belz as part of the commemoration of the two hundredth anniversary of the Constitution over two decades ago. The goal remains the same. The essays are intended to provide both students and teachers with brief, accessible, and reliable introductions to some of the most important aspects of American constitutional development. The essays reflect the leading scholarship in the field and address topics that are classic, timely, and always important.

American constitutionalism is characterized by a series of tensions. Such tensions are persistent features of American constitutional history, and they make a frequent appearance in these essays. The American tradition emphasizes the importance of written constitutions. The United States Constitution declares that "this Constitution" is the "supreme law of the land." But time moves on. Politics and society are ever changing. How do we manage the tension between being faithful to a written constitutional text and adapting to changing political circumstances? To the extent that the American brand of constitutionalism binds us to the past, creates stability, and slows political change, how do we balance these conservative forces with the pressures of the moment that might demand departures from inherited ways of doing things and old ideas about rights and values? We sometimes change the terms of the old text through amendment or wholesale replacement of one constitution with another (from the Articles of Confederation to the Constitution at the national level, or more often at the state level), but we apply and adapt the inherited constitutional text through interpretation and practice. All the while, we manage the tension between being faithful to the text that we have and embracing the "living constitution" that grows out of that text.

Law figures prominently in the American constitutional tradition. Our written constitutions are understood to be fundamental laws and part of our legal code. They are the foundation of our legal system and superior to all other laws. They provide legally enforceable rules for judges and others to follow. Judges and lawyers play an important role in interpreting American constitutions and translating the bare bones of the original text into the detailed body of doctrine known as constitutional law. It has often been the dream of judges, lawyers, and legal scholars to insulate constitutional law from the world of politics. There is a long-held aspiration for judges and lawyers to be able to spin out constitutional law in accord with established principles of justice, reason, and tradition. But politics has also been central to the history of American constitutionalism. Constitutions are created by political actors and serve political purposes. Once in place, constitutional rules and values are politically contested, and they are interpreted and put into practice by politicians and political activists, as well as by judges. The tension between law and politics is a persistent one in American constitutional history.

A final tension of note has been between power and liberty. In the modern tradition, constitutional government is limited government. Constitutions impose limits and create mechanisms for making those constraints effective. They specify what the boundaries of government power are and what rights individuals and groups have against government. But there is also an older tradition, in which constitutions organize and empower government. The US Constitution contains both elements. Many of its provisions, especially the amendments, limit government. These are some of the most celebrated features of the Constitution, and they have become the basis for much of the constitutional law that has been developed by the judiciary. But the Constitution was specifically adopted to empower the federal government and create new, better institutions that could accomplish national objectives. Both the US Constitution and the state constitutions are designed to gather and direct government power to advance the public good. Throughout American constitutional history, judges, politicians, and activists have struggled over the proper balance between empowering government and limiting government and over the best understanding of the rights of individuals and the public welfare.

These essays examine American constitutionalism, not a particular constitutional text. The US Constitution figures prominently in these essays, as it does in American history, but the American constitutional tradition includes other foundational documents, including notably the state constitutions. These texts are a guide to the subject matter of these essays, but they are not exhaustive of it. Laws, court decisions, administrative actions, and custom, along with founding documents, perform constitutional functions in the American political system, just as they do in the British system where there is no single written "constitution." Whether "written" or "unwritten," constitutions perform certain common tasks.

Constitutions define the organic structures of government, specifying the basic institutions for making and implementing public policy, including the processes for altering the constitution itself. Constitutions distribute powers among those institutions of government, delegating, enumerating, prohibiting, and reserving powers to each governmental body. The flip side of entrusting power and discretion to governmental bodies is the definition of limits on those powers, the specification of individual and collective rights. Constitutions also specify who participates in the institutions of government and how and to whom the power of government applies. That is, constitutions identify the structures of citizenship and political jurisdiction. Across its seven articles and twenty-seven amendments, the US Constitution addresses all of these topics, but the text is only a starting point. These topics form the subject matter of New Essays on American Constitutional History.

Writing early in the twentieth century, the great constitutional historian Edward Corwin observed that relatively few citizens actually read the US Constitution, despite its brevity. He thought that this was in part because the "real constitution of the United States has come to mean something very different from the document" itself. The document laid out the framework of government, but "the real scope of the powers which it should exercise and of the rights which it should guarantee was left, to a very great extent, for future developments to determine." Understanding American constitutionalism requires understanding American constitutional history. It is a history of contestation and change, creation and elaboration. These essays aim to illuminate that history.

—*Keith E. Whittington*
Princeton University

—*Gerry Leonard*
Boston University School of Law

Introduction: A Union of Republics in a Predatory World

Early in the summer of 1783, George Washington concluded that the military and political situation at last allowed him to tender his resignation as commander in chief of the Continental army. After eight long years the American War of Independence was over, and George III had reluctantly acknowledged that his erstwhile colonies were now independent states. As the central leader in the struggle against Britain, Washington felt obliged to add to his letter of resignation a few "sentiments respecting some important subjects which appear[ed] to [him] to be intimately connected with the tranquility of the United States." Washington's sentiments offer a snapshot of the political circumstances of the newly independent United States, a nation that from then on had to make its own way in the world. His letter can therefore serve as a useful starting point from which to begin an investigation into the nature of the American union and the challenges that led to the Philadelphia Convention and the creation of the Constitution in 1787.

Washington addressed his letter of resignation neither to Congress nor to the American people but to the governors of the thirteen states, asking them to relay his sentiments to their respective legislatures. This is a poignant reminder of where both formal and de facto power resided in the United States in 1783. Washington served a union of thirteen republics, not a nation-state or an American people. The future of this union and its role in maintaining the liberty and independence of its member states were the core concerns of his circular. As commander in chief of the American army, Washington had witnessed at close range the defects of the union and its inability to organize and pursue the War of Independence in an efficient manner. "I could demonstrate to every mind open to conviction," he wrote,

> that in less time & with much less expence than has been incurred, the War might have been brought to the same happy, conclusion if the resources of the Continent could have been properly drawn forth—that the distresses and disappointments, which have very often occurred, have

In too many instances resulted more from a want of
energy in the Continental Government, than a deficiency
of means in the particular States—That the inefficacy of
measures, arising from the want of an adequate authority
in the supreme Power, from a partial compliance with
the requisitions of Congress in some of the States and
from a failure of punctuality in others, while it tended to
damp the Zeal of those which where [sic] more willing to
exert themselves, served also to accumulate the expences
of the War and to frustrate the best concerted plans.

Washington was describing the administration of union affairs under the
Articles of Confederation and the lack of effective power in what contempo-
raries referred to as the "general" government. No one doubted the need
for such a government. It was "indispensible to the happiness of the
individual States that there should be lodged somewhere, a supreme power
to regulate and govern the general concerns of the confederated Republic,"
Washington wrote. But unless the states would allow Congress "to exercise
those prerogatives" invested in it by the confederation articles, "every thing
must very rapidly tend to Anarchy and confusion."

Washington's words echoed a growing concern among a group of
politicians who had been closely involved in directing the war against
Britain that the American union was on the road to dissolution. "Anarchy
and confusion" was eighteenth-century shorthand for the civil wars and
domestic disturbances many observers foresaw should the union disintegrate
into a North American state system in which thirteen unconnected republics
would vie for supremacy and reproduce the interstate tensions and conflicts
that were typical of contemporary Europe. Ultimately, disunion spelled the
end to both liberty and independence. Anarchy would compel the people
to support any tyrant who promised to restore order, even if the cost were
giving up popular liberties. Independence could be maintained only if
foreign predatory nations could be kept at bay. But without a strong and
effective union the American states would become "the sport of European
Politicks." The great powers of the Old World would "play one State against
another" to prevent the "growing importance" of America and "to serve
their own interested purposes."

Despite his anxiety about the union's future, Washington's letter fell short
of formulating a program for the reform of the Articles of Confederation.
He was content to merely highlight two specific concerns. The first was the
need to honor the debts to public creditors, army officers, and wounded
veterans that the union had incurred fighting the War of Independence. The

second was the need to provide for the defense of the United States by setting up an efficient military peace establishment. In addition to an "indissoluble Union of the States under one federal Head," justice to creditors, officers, and soldiers, and a viable peace establishment, Washington added one more thing that he believed "essential to the well being" and even "to the existence, of the United States as an independent Power": a readiness of the American people to set aside state interests in favor of the common good of the union. Yet he offered no recipe for cultivating that readiness but left it "to the good sense and serious consideration of those immediately concerned." Those most "immediately concerned" were of course the very same state governors and state legislators who were the recipients of Washington's letter and on whose actions the future of the union now depended.[1]

Washington's missive reflected concerns about the needs and shortcomings of the American union that reform politicians would repeatedly identify and air between the conclusion of the War of Independence and the adoption of the Constitution. Although political union was a prerequisite for the preservation of liberty and independence, the union was under constant strain from the fallout of the War of Independence. Common obligations had been incurred during the war, and independence created a range of problems that the American colonies had not faced as dependents of the British Empire. The pressure from common obligations and external forces caused political tension because the United States was a confederation of thirteen heterogeneous republics, each of which reacted differently to the same stimulus. A constant balancing act between the need for union, on the one hand, and the interests of the states, on the other, therefore became the distinctive feature of national politics in the early United States.

I. An Internationalist Interpretation of the Founding of the United States

American historians have always regarded the years between the signing of the Peace of Paris in September 1783, which ended the War of Independence, and the framing of the new federal Constitution four years later, as a particularly important period in the nation's history. The peace treaty signaled Britain's acceptance of the bid for independence that the colonies had made on July 4, 1776. Yet to many historians it was the Constitution, rather than the Peace of Paris, that secured independence and thereby served as the ending point of the American Revolution. The new nation had faced many difficulties after the conclusion of the war with Britain, and the Constitution was the means to resolve them. Popular authors and commentators who celebrate the achievements of the so-called Founding Fathers also typically embrace this view. Most historians, however, are much more critical of the Constitution. To them, the framing and adoption of the Constitution meant the destruction of egalitarian and democratic promises introduced by the American Revolution.

Both views have impressive pedigrees that can be traced all the way back to the founding generation. Yet the discussion among modern historians owes more to works published in the late nineteenth and early twentieth centuries, when history was becoming an academic discipline. In 1888, the lawyer-turned-philosopher and historian John Fiske published an essay in which he argued that "the period of five years following the peace of 1783 was the most critical moment in all the history of the American people. The dangers from which we were saved in 1788 were even greater than the dangers from which we were saved in 1865." Although his book is rarely read today, Fiske made a lasting contribution to American historiography by popularizing the term *critical period*, first used by John Quincy Adams in his 1787 Harvard valedictory address, in reference to the 1780s. Fiske's account of the dangers of the critical period also subsequently made its way into monographs and textbooks that shaped perceptions of the period.[2]

To Fiske, the core problem facing the new nation was its dysfunctional central government, which was unable to meet challenges to American sovereignty and national interests. But while it was a major problem that Congress was weak and the union fragile, this state of affairs was hardly surprising. In the aftermath of independence, most Americans still identified with their own states rather than with the United States. Without a common sense of nationality, there was no popular basis for a movement to firm up the union and build a stronger national government. In fact, the thirteen states had come together only to defend their independence against Britain. Once that conflict was resolved, the natural tendency was for their union to disintegrate into its foundational elements, the states. At the same time, the states shared a number of concerns that served like a centripetal force to counterbalance the centrifugal tendency to disintegration.

Perhaps the most fundamental reason to stay united was that the United States was recognized as one nation, rather than thirteen republics, by the monarchies and empires of Europe. That the center of this nation was weak was evident already in the peace treaty that created it. Several passages of the Paris treaty spoke not of what the United States would do as a signatory but of what Congress would "earnestly recommend . . . the legislatures of the respective states" do. Although foreign powers often doubted the United States' ability to live up to treaty obligations, in the context of the law of nations, the American union was nevertheless regarded as one nation. Another incitement to continued union lay in the western reaches of the nation. Several of the states had ceded territorial claims west of the Appalachian Mountains to Congress, creating a vast public domain north of the Ohio River that was administered by Congress, not the states. When the Constitutional Convention met, this was a new development, but there was widespread expectation that the region would absorb thousands of settlers from the thirteen states and from Europe in years to come. Finally, the struggle for independence had left a legacy of shared obligations in the form of a large foreign and domestic debt contracted by Congress in the name of the United States. Defaulting on these debt obligations would cause moral as well as economic and political problems. Quite apart from these tangible causes for continued union, there was also reason to think that the states would be more successful in defending and promoting their interests both in North America and on the Atlantic Ocean as a federal union than they would be as thirteen separate republics.[3]

But if there were good reasons for the states to continue in the union, their Articles of Confederation had not established a central government with sufficient strength to manage their common concerns. In a list often repeated since, Fiske identified a number of areas where Congress could not fulfill international obligations or stand up for American interests: Congress could not enforce international treaties, principally the peace treaty; it could not force the British to abandon military posts on United States soil held contrary to the treaty; it could not adopt countermeasures against Britain's discrimination against American shipping or Spain's closure of the Mississippi River to American traders; it could not impose a common navigation act on the states; it could not prevent conflicts between the states over interstate commerce (among other incidents, Fiske claimed that New York's customs duties deliberately discriminated against New Jersey and Connecticut traders) and territorial boundaries (Connecticut and Pennsylvania clashed over the Wyoming Valley, New York and New Hampshire over the Green Mountains); it could not service its foreign debt or secure new loans on good terms; it could not retaliate against the Barbary States' depredations on American trade in the Mediterranean; it could not secure the loyalty of citizens in Kentucky and New England who contemplated secession, and so on.

In Fiske's account, the Philadelphia Convention came together to address these challenges, and in the absence of a popular movement for reform of the union and the national government, he naturally came to stress the role of influential statesmen rather than the people out of doors in bringing about reform. Fiske called the Constitution the "Iliad, or Parthenon, or Fifth Symphony, of statesmanship," revealing not only his admiration for the work of the founders, but his belief that they were selfless politicians hoping to promote the common good. Although Fiske's narrative ended with the inauguration of George Washington as first president in April 1789, the implication of his work was that the new federal government under Washington's lead defused the dangers of the critical period. The Constitution thereby ensured that the national independence that was declared in name in 1776 became a reality in 1789.[4]

Fiske wrote his essay a century after the founding and two decades after the Civil War, at a time when sectional conflict and international weakness had an immediacy now long lost. Neither continued union nor international great power status was taken for granted by Fiske, and the consequences of disunion were very real to him. In a passage grounded in equal measures in his evolutionary theory of history and his triumphant Anglo-Saxonism, Fiske wrote that the fortunate outcome of the "critical period" had determined that "the continent of North America should be dominated by a single powerful and pacific federal nation instead of being parcelled out among forty or fifty small communities, wasting their strength and lowering their moral tone by perpetual warfare, like the states of ancient Greece, or by perpetual preparation for warfare, like the nations of modern Europe."[5]

A quarter century after the publication of Fiske's essay, there appeared a work in many ways its inversion, which has ever since exercised enormous influence on historians' understanding of the nation's founding. Whereas Fiske saw the 1780s as a period of interstate and international rivalries, Charles Beard's *An Economic Interpretation of the Constitution of the United States* concentrated on domestic struggles between social groups representing antagonistic interests. Beard and his followers in the so-called progressive school of interpretation deemphasized the problem of independence and argued that the fears over disunion and international depredations so often raised by the founding generation were no more than a ruse. The crucial question at the heart of the founding was not whether the United States would remain independent, but what sort of society it would become. In the progressive interpretation, the founding was a struggle over the distribution of scarce resources, and the Constitution was the means by which one class gained control over the central government to further its own material interests.

Whereas Fiske's approach downplayed the opposition to the Constitution— he dismissed anti-federalism as "purely a policy of negation and obstruction," for example—Charles Beard, with Mary Beard, argued that the Constitution was adopted not by the American people but by an interested segment of the population: "Broadly speaking, the division of the voters over the document ran along economic lines. The merchants, manufacturers, private creditors, and holders of public securities loomed large among the advocates of the new system, while the opposition came chiefly from the small farmers behind the seaboard, especially from the men who, in earlier years, had demanded paper money and other apparatus for easing the strain of their debts."[6]

It followed from the Beards' analysis of the struggle over ratification that they approached the idea of a critical period with considerable skepticism. "When it is remembered," Charles Beard asserts in his *Economic Interpretation*, "that most of our history has been written by Federalists, it will become apparent that great care should be taken in accepting, without reserve, the gloomy pictures of the social conditions prevailing under the Articles of Confederation." In fact, the critical period was little more than "a phantom of the imagination." Although the Beards accepted that some socioeconomic groups, essentially those who supported the Constitution, suffered in the 1780s, they ventured the guess that the country as a whole "was in many respects steadily recovering order and prosperity even under the despised Articles of Confederation."[7]

Despite his reputation as an iconoclast, Beard's analysis of the founding was in fact always restrained. A much more uncompromising attitude was adopted by Merrill Jensen, a historian thirty years Beard's junior who has also been extremely influential among his peers. Not only did Jensen claim that the 1780s was a period of "extraordinary economic growth," he also made explicit the struggle over democracy that was only implicit in Beard's work. To Jensen, the revolutionary era was dominated by a struggle between "radicals" and "conservatives," which followed on "the democratization of the American society by the destruction of the coercive authority of Great Britain and the establishment of actual local self-government within the separate states under the Articles of Confederation." Jensen's radicals were democrats and supporters of state sovereignty, while his conservatives were aristocrats and nationalists. Whereas the Declaration of Independence and the Articles of Confederation were the institutional manifestations of radical ideals, the Constitution was the work of the conservatives. The Federalists, said Jensen, "engineered a conservative counter-revolution and erected a nationalistic government whose purpose in part was to thwart the will of 'the people' in whose name they acted."[8]

For most of the twentieth century, the tradition established by Beard and Jensen has dominated scholarship on the creation of the Constitution. The founding has been interpreted as a struggle between social classes over issues arising primarily within, rather than outside, the United States. This holds true also for the work that for the last five decades has served as the standard interpretation of the period between the Peace of Paris and the adoption of the Constitution, Gordon Wood's *Creation of the American Republic*. But in recent years there has been a renewed interest in the twinned questions of federalism and international relations that featured so prominently in Fiske's account of the critical period. Such "internationalist" interpretations, in contrast to the economic interpretations of the progressives, reflect a general turn in the profession that has compelled historians to analyze the many ways in which separate national histories are connected to, or entangled with, one another. Peter Onuf and David Armitage have written about the international and global history of the Declaration of Independence. David Golove and Daniel Hulsebosch have interpreted the Constitution as "a fundamentally international document"—not a counterrevolutionary negation of the promise of the Declaration but a continuation of its attempt to secure international recognition of the fledgling United States. Eliga Gould has presented a similar argument, showing how American statesmen struggled to make their new nation assume its rank "among the powers of the earth." Robbie Totten has argued that the Constitution was the solution to a two-sided diplomatic crisis of how to work out the relationship between the thirteen new American republics and their collective relationship to foreign powers. Leonard Sadosky has pointed to the importance of settling the new nation's relationship not only with European states and empires but also with Native American nations in order to secure the promises of independence.[9]

These newer works point to international and intra-union, rather than domestic, relations in their analysis of both the causes and the consequences of the Constitution. And rather than competition between classes, they point to competition between polities as the main driver of political development. International interpretations therefore call for a return to, and a reassessment of, the so-called dual revolution thesis that progressive historians have used to make sense of the American nation-building process. The term *dual revolution* was coined by a contemporary of Beard, Carl Becker, to capture how the American founding was at the same time "a struggle for home rule," or independence, and "a struggle over who should rule at home," or, in Becker's words, a struggle over "the democratization of American politics and society." Although the progressive tradition has never denied the significance of independence, it has always emphasized the struggle over democratization as the more important development. Representing a return to Fiske's approach, international interpretations reverse this priority by arguing that neither political independence nor the creation of a stable federal union were foregone conclusions of the American Revolution.[10]

The following pages draw on the insights of scholars who have studied foreign affairs and federalism in the founding era to present the framing and ratification of the Constitution as the outcome of a perceived need to secure the survival of the American union of republics as an independent nation. Multiple challenges arose from the American colonies' transition to independent nationhood, and the conviction rapidly grew that these challenges could not be effectively addressed within the framework of the Articles of Confederation. By 1787, the American states faced the choice of either reinvigorating their union or dissolving it. Both main routes contained alternatives. Many people who accepted the need for reform still believed that the best way to make the American union fit for purpose was to amend the Articles of Confederation. Others came to think that a completely new compact of union had to be substituted for the old. Similarly, the dissolution of the union did not necessarily mean that the states would be on their own. A more common projection was for the existing union of thirteen states to be replaced by two or three smaller regional confederations of economically and culturally more homogeneous sections. The outcome of the political crisis of the confederation was therefore not preordained. Nor does the Constitution represent the realization of a single master plan. Rather it was shaped by an extended debate and repeated compromises in which the need for union to preserve the independence and well-being of the states confronted and sometimes clashed with the impulse to defend state and sectional identities and interests.

The perspective shift provided by an international interpretation of the founding raises the question whether scholars have mischaracterized both the Constitution and the American union and thereby exaggerated the degree to which the founding generation sought to radically recast early American social and political life. This does not mean that the questions raised by previous interpretations are without value. To the contrary, and perhaps counterintuitively, a reinterpretation of the Constitution's origins that emphasizes the importance of home rule in fact allows for a fresh look also at the old progressive question of who should rule at home once American independence was secured, and thus for a reinvigoration of the tradition of constitutional analysis initiated by Beard and others well over a century ago.

II. Articles of Confederation and Perpetual Union

Only rarely do attempts to capture the meaning of the Constitution begin in the actual text of the compact. This is a missed opportunity, because the key to the document's interpretation is present in plain sight already in the preamble. The Constitution was presented to "the people" of the American states for their adoption or rejection. In an age of poor communication, with no national newspapers or other media, the framers had every reason to let the charter itself speak as clearly as possible about their aspirations. Thus, the Committee of Style, appointed at the Philadelphia Convention, introduced the Constitution with the declaration that its aim was "to form a more perfect union." The preamble would therefore suggest that the most fruitful way to unravel the meaning of the Constitution should take the form of an investigation of the concept of union. At the same time, the wording "more perfect" signals that the Constitution has to be analyzed alongside the imperfections of the compact of union that preceded it, the Articles of Confederation.

In the history of the American union, the transition from the Articles of Confederation to the Constitution is a story of both change and continuity. Adoption of the Constitution signified important changes to both the legitimating principles and the structure of the union. The authority of the Constitution rested on popular sovereignty, whereas the Articles of Confederation had been an agreement between the states. In contrast to the articles, the Constitution was adopted by the people of the states, through their representatives in special state ratifying conventions, rather than the state governments. The Constitution also created a national government that could act independently of the states, whereas the Continental Congress had depended on the state governments to execute its decisions. Furthermore, the Constitution invested in Congress new powers to regulate commerce and to tax, and it circumscribed certain powers of the states, most significantly by forbidding them from issuing paper money and from "impairing the obligation of contracts." But in other respects there was continuity. The principle remained that the union and the national government were designed primarily to govern the common affairs of the states—e.g., interstate matters, the western territories, and foreign affairs, including commerce—rather than the domestic affairs of the states. As a leading political theorist has put it, the framers were critical of the confederation for "its failure to achieve the ends for which it was instituted, not its failure to reach ends beyond these." Nor did the Constitution challenge the principle that the union was primarily a political organization meant to further the interests of the states. Despite significant changes, the Constitution should therefore be seen first and foremost as a reform of the organization of the federal union, not of its rationale or aims.[11]

Federal union was a well-known term in eighteenth-century political discourse, used to describe the means whereby weak states could safeguard their sovereignty. Its rationale was security. States associated in a federal union to preserve peace among themselves and to provide protection from external aggression. Republics in particular were inclined to confederate because they were smaller and weaker than monarchies and faced different security concerns. In a chapter entitled "How republics provide for their security," Montesquieu's *Spirit of the Laws* described a federal union, in words frequently cited by Americans, as "a kind of constitution that has all the internal advantages of republican government and the external force of monarchy." It was "a society of societies," composed of republics that enjoyed "the goodness of the internal government of each one," yet which, "with regard to the exterior," had "by the force of the association, all the advantages of large monarchies." In another influential treatise, *The Law of Nations*, Emer de Vattel explained that a federal union was a political organization that bound together states that had voluntarily restrained the exercise of their sovereignty to better preserve their standing as independent states. A federal republic allowed republics to provide for their security needs by investing a common council with powers over war and diplomacy and the authority to act on their behalf in the international state system.[12]

Inherent in the concept of federal union was the principle of a division of governmental duties and authorities between a confederation government and the governments of the member states. This division followed the distinction conventionally made by early modern political theorists between international and domestic governmental affairs. There was no universally accepted nomenclature, however. John Locke used the terms "executive" and "federative" powers, with the latter referring to "the management of the *security and interest of the publick without*, with all those that it may receive benefit and damage from," including "the Power of War and Peace, Leagues and Alliances, and all the Transactions with all Persons and Communities without the Commonwealth." Montesquieu instead spoke of two forms of executive power, one pertaining to "the things depending on civil right" and the other to "the things depending on the right of nations." By means of the latter form of executive power, he wrote, the magistrate "makes peace or war, sends or receives embassies, establishes security, and prevents invasions." When they entered into union, states delegated the exercise of their federative powers, or, in Montesquieu's words, their executive power pertaining to "the things depending on the right of nations," to a common confederation government.[13]

When American constitutional commentators of the founding generation looked back at the origins of the United States, they agreed that security and international relations had been the main rationales behind the formation of the American union. In the early years of the 1790s, James Wilson, a Federalist, paraphrased Montesquieu, saying that the federal republic combined the "vigour and decision of a wide-spreading monarchy" with "the freedom and beneficence of a compacted commonwealth." A decade later, St. George Tucker, a Jeffersonian, wrote that like every other confederation the American union was "chiefly founded upon this circumstance, that each people choose to remain their own masters, and yet are not strong enough to make a head against a common enemy." The primacy of security was put more bluntly by a congressional committee report from early 1781 that dealt with the need for stronger union. The origins of the American "Confederate Republic," it said, lay in the need "to crush the pr[esent] & future foes of her Independence."[14]

The principle that union was a necessary means for independence—i.e., that the states had to restrict their sovereignty to guarantee it—became the first axiom of American political theory. In the struggle against Britain in the early 1770s, several people who would go on to become leading statesmen developed what historians have termed a "commonwealth" conception of the British Empire. They stressed the corporate status and rights of the colonies against the right of Parliament to legislate for Britain's American dependencies, and they argued that the empire was a conglomeration of sovereign polities held together by their voluntary subjection to the rule of the British monarch. They thereby came to depict the British Empire as a kind of federal union. When the time came to create a union of independent states, their understanding of the British Empire would influence their work. A "state," a youthful Alexander Hamilton wrote in his *Farmer Refuted*, could be understood as "a number of individual societies, or bodies politic, united under one common head." In the British Empire it was "the person and prerogative of the King . . . that conjoins all these individual societies, into one great body politic," doing so "to preserve their mutual connexion and dependence, and make them all co-operate to one common end the general good." Thomas Jefferson told a similar story. On

emigrating to America, he claimed, Englishmen had chosen to "continue
their union" with the mother country "by submitting themselves to the
same common sovereign, who was thereby made the central link connecting
the several parts of the empire thus newly multiplied." Under the penname
"Novanglus," John Adams argued that the colonies were sovereign polities
equipped with their own legislative assemblies that "have, and ought to
exercise, every power of the house of Commons."[15]

The commonwealth concept of imperial organization accepted that
Parliament had the right to regulate trade within and without the British
Empire. But this arrangement, Adams said, "may be compared to a treaty of
commerce, by which those distinct states are cemented together, in perpetual
league and amity." In other words, it did not negate the corporate identity
and interests of the American polities. At least in the abstract Adams seems
to have accepted the potential problem that states might pursue their own
"particular interests" to the detriment of the common good of the whole.
A "superintending power" might therefore be necessary to ensure that all
states acted in concert, at least in the event of war or commercial conflicts.
Nevertheless, Adams claimed that serious conflicts of interests were unlikely
and called for the continuation of the status quo "by letting parliament
regulate trade and our own assemblies all other matters."[16]

The notion that Britain's American colonies were in effect self-governing
polities bound together in union with the mother country for purposes of
trade and defense also colored the flurry of formal plans for imperial reform
that appeared as the imperial crisis unfolded in the 1770s. According to one
count there were as many as thirty-seven plans between the years 1774 and
1777 alone. On the Loyalist side, the Philadelphia merchant and politician
Joseph Galloway authored the most important plan. In the opposing camp,
Benjamin Franklin wrote one and Silas Deane two, the first on his own
and the other with his fellow Connecticut delegates to Congress. These
plans shed much light on how Americans perceived the purposes of union,
whether it was the union of the British imperial commonwealth or a union
of American independent states. They also show how indeterminate the
concept of union was in this early phase of the struggle for independence.[17]

Galloway, Franklin, and Deane all adopted the familiar distinction
between internal and external powers. They proposed that Locke's
"federative" powers be delegated to a union by the American states, but
carefully preserved other powers in the colonial assemblies. As a Loyalist,
Galloway suggested that a "Grand Council" of American colonies would
have the right to administer intercolonial affairs and relations with Britain
but that Parliament would continue to manage defense and trade. In his

scheme, each colony was to "retain its present Constitution and powers of regulating and governing its own internal Police in all Cases whatsoever." Rarely used today, the term *internal police* was common in late eighteenth-century political and social discourse. Derived from the ancient Greek word *πολιτεία* (politeia) over the French *police* and often rendered "policy" or "policie" in English, *internal police* referred to a wide and eclectic range of government regulations of health, morals, education, communications, and the economy, covering virtually everything an eighteenth-century government did domestically apart from taxation and the administration of justice. The term could therefore serve as convenient shorthand for the powers over which American statesmen envisaged the colonies and states would retain full control, even after they had delegated their "federative" powers to the union.

Franklin, Deane, and the Connecticut delegation promoted the creation of "a firm League of Friendship" among the colonies, to provide "for their common Defence, against their Enemies, for the Security of their Liberties and Propertys, the Safety of their Persons and Families, and their mutual and general Welfare." An American "General Congress" would have power to declare war and peace; to send and receive ambassadors; to enter into alliances with foreign powers; to arbitrate intercolonial conflicts; to create new colonies; and to administer affairs with Native American nations. Congress would also make ordinances necessary to "the General Welfare," a term that would later cause much concern among states' rights advocates. But Franklin explained that "general welfare" referred only to the management of international commerce, currency, and the military. Like Galloway, Franklin proposed that the American states would be self-governing in domestic matters. Every member of the union would "enjoy and retain as much as it may think fit of its own present Laws, Customs, Rights, Privileges, and peculiar Jurisdictions within its own Limits; and may amend its own Constitution as shall seem best to its own Assembly or Convention." Deane's own plan and that of the Connecticut delegation added that every confederate would "have the sole direction and government of its own internal police."[18]

The concept of a union of self-governing states delegating authority over international and interstate matters to a common council reflects the understanding that the colonies were sovereign polities. Yet many of the details of their confederation were not worked out at this early stage. The plans are surprisingly vague about the need for the states to be represented as distinctive bodies politic in Congress, for example. Most authors proposed representation proportional to population and delegates voting as individuals. Only the Connecticut plan insisted that representatives should vote both as individuals and as state delegations. The implication of these recommendations is that Franklin and others imagined a Congress that represented an American people rather than thirteen sovereign states. But it is not clear whether this was a carefully considered position or not. If it was, it found few supporters in Congress.

Neither Deane nor Franklin was a member of the congressional committee that drew up the first American compact of union. Leading this task was John Dickinson, a veteran of the pamphlet wars against the British Parliament but a reluctant convert to independence. The Articles of Confederation were long in the making. On June 7, 1776, Richard Henry Lee, acting on instructions from the Virginia assembly, moved that the American colonies "are, and of right ought to be, free and independent States" and that their political connection with Britain should be dissolved. Lee's motion called for a declaration of independence but also asked Congress to form foreign military alliances against the mother country and to prepare "a plan of confederation." Congress quickly appointed a committee to draw up a declaration of independence and another to "prepare and digest the form of confederation to be entered into between these colonies." After a few weeks, Dickinson's committee presented to Congress a first draft, which was debated, amended, and recommitted. A second report followed in the summer of 1777, but pressing matters postponed the adoption of an amended version until November 15. Ten states then ratified it within five months, but Delaware, Maryland, and New Jersey delayed action. Although the articles served as the de facto compact of union, they were not formally adopted until ratified by Maryland in February 1781.[19]

Thomas Burke of North Carolina was the first member of Congress to articulate a full-fledged view of the American union as a confederation among sovereign states that had delegated only *expressly enumerated* powers to a common national council. As Congress debated the draft Articles of Confederation, his view that the union was created by the states through a voluntary restriction of their sovereignty gradually took hold. The success of this concept of the union in overcoming ideas implicit in earlier plans can be seen in the stipulation in the fifth article in the Articles of Confederation that each state, regardless of size, had one vote in Congress, and in the thirteenth article, which demanded unanimous agreement by all states to any alteration of the articles. It has often been pointed out that Article XIII gave each state a veto on amendment proposals. But far from an oversight, this right was necessary if the articles were to be a compact among sovereign states, which by definition could be altered only by the unanimous consent of all contracting parties. That the articles were in fact regarded as such a compact is evident from Article II, which stated: "Each state retains its sovereignty, freedom and independence, and every Power, Jurisdiction and right, which is not by this confederation expressly delegated to the United States, in Congress assembled."[20]

The full title of the agreement between the American states, habitually referred to as the Articles of Confederation, was "Articles of Confederation and Perpetual Union." Although seldom commented upon, the second part of the title is as important as the first. Dickinson's committee was well versed in the law of nations and no doubt picked a name that would correctly convey the nature of the American compact. In his highly influential treatise *Of the Law of Nature and of Nations*, Samuel von Pufendorf had explained that what he called "systems" of states could be formed either by the common subjection of states under the same monarch or "when two or more States are linked together in one Body by virtue of some League or Alliance." The "commonwealth" concept of the British Empire was an example of the former system. Pufendorf called the latter type "perpetual" leagues to distinguish them from temporary agreements between sovereign nations that did not aim to establish "any lasting Union, as to the chief Management of Affairs." The "chief Occasion" for the formation of perpetual leagues was the by now familiar recognition "that each particular People loved to be their own Masters, and yet each was not strong enough to make Head against a Common Enemy." When entering into a perpetual alliance for these purposes, states agreed not to "exercise some part of the Sovereignty . . . without the General Consent of each other." The most important powers that states in a perpetual alliance ceded to their confederacy were "the Affair[s] of Peace and War" that could henceforth be exercised only with "the general consent of the whole Confederacy."[21]

As adopted, the Articles of Confederation conformed even better to Pufendorf's ideas of perpetual leagues and alliances than did the Dickinson committee drafts. Article III stated that "the said states hereby severally enter into a firm league of friendship with each other, for their common defence, the security of their Liberties, and their mutual and general welfare, binding themselves to assist each other, against all force offered to, or attacks made upon them, or any of them, on account of religion, sovereignty, trade, or any pretence whatever." The states ceded their "federative powers" to a Congress of states, which was given exclusive power over war and peace, treaties and alliances with foreign powers, the exchange of ambassadors, the creation and regulation of prize courts and courts trying felonies committed on the high seas, and the issuing of letters of marque and reprisal. Dickinson's first draft prevented the states from levying trade duties that interfered with the union's commercial treaties. But opposition from states' rights advocates meant that the final version of the articles compromised Congress's ability to pursue an effective commercial policy by stipulating that "no treaty of commerce shall be made, whereby the legislative power of the respective states shall be restrained from imposing such imposts and duties on foreigners, as their own people are subjected to, or from prohibiting the exportation or importation of any species of goods or commodities whatsoever" (Article IX).[22]

By amending the original Dickinson plan, Congress also rolled back many of the powers over interstate arbitration and the western lands that Dickinson's committee would have delegated to the general government and which would eventually be restored to the federal government in 1787 by the Northwest Ordinance and the Constitution. But the adopted Articles of Confederation carefully guarded the sovereignty of the states by restricting congressional intervention in interstate conflicts to situations in which a state had petitioned for arbitration. In the West, the adopted articles stopped short of investing Congress with an exclusive right to regulate Native American affairs. Instead, Congress was granted the right of "regulating the trade and managing all affairs with the Indians, not members of any of the states; provided that the legislative right of any state, within its own limits, be not infringed or violated," a formulation that left diplomacy with Native American nations open to competition between the national government and the states.[23]

The articles also conformed to Pufendorf's concept of a perpetual league by reserving for the confederating states the power over internal matters, with only a few exceptions. Congress was given authority to create a common market by regulating coinage and the standards of weights and measures and by managing the postal service. Interstate exchange was also facilitated by the interstate comity stipulations in Article IV. This article guaranteed freedom of movement by granting to "the free inhabitants of each of these states, paupers, vagabonds and fugitives from Justice excepted . . . all privileges and immunities of free citizens in the several states" as well as "free ingress and regress to and from any other state" together with "the privileges of trade and commerce, subject to the same duties, impositions and restrictions as the inhabitants thereof respectively, provided that such restriction shall not extend so far as to prevent the removal of property imported into any state, to any other State of which the Owner is an inhabitant." But all other domestic matters were left to the states to order as they saw fit.

The origins of the first American federal union, institutionalized in the Articles of Confederation, suggests that it is best understood as an organizational solution to security concerns that allowed thirteen small and weak republics to join together to defend their independence and interests. In accordance with the precepts of early modern political theorists, the American union invested powers over war and international matters in a congress of states, but the state governments retained their right to govern their own internal affairs. Despite the fact that Congress was charged with very extensive duties, the Articles of Confederation created little in the way of national governmental institutions. Nor did the articles create a sovereign American people. They provided no method to collect the popular will outside the thirteen states. Hence, although the United States became a "nation" within the international system of states, and in the eyes of the law of nations that governed it, the American union did not become a nation-state. As a result, there could be no national will separate from the interests of the member states. At the same time, there was always awareness that the union was necessary for the states to survive and flourish as independent polities. To a degree not always appreciated, this understanding of the federal union survived the transition from the Articles of Confederation to the Constitution.

III. THE CRITICAL PERIOD OF THE 1780s

The Articles of Confederation were written to better organize the armed struggle against Britain and to signal to European powers that the American states were serious in their pursuit of independence. Though the articles provided for de facto union upon their adoption by Congress in 1777, the politics of state interest nevertheless delayed formal ratification until 1781, when the war was all but over. During the conflict, the articles fell considerably short of their intended aim. Once the war ended, and Britain recognized American independence, securing state compliance with decisions of Congress proved even harder than during the struggle against Britain. By the middle of the 1780s, the United States faced a number of challenges that called into question the viability of the existing union. These challenges are most easily appreciated by focusing on the two geographic zones where the new American states interacted with the outside world: the Atlantic marketplace and the western borderlands. Economic historians believe that the standard of living in the free white population of North America was the highest in the world on the eve of the Revolution, and the colonists were accustomed to continuous economic growth. But their wealth was in large part based on easy access to new agricultural land and foreign markets. Once liberated from the British Empire, the new nation could provide neither.

Important sectors of the American economy were heavily trade-dependent, and the colonists had flourished in the extensive common market of the British Empire. Yet they expected to do even better once freed from the shackles of Britain's mercantilist policies. However, such hopes were put to shame when expulsion from the empire instead caused a severe economic shock. Exports fell by as much as a quarter compared to pre-Revolution volumes, despite a rapidly growing population. As a result the economy slowed. According to one economic historian, the War of Independence may have set back gross domestic product per capita by as much as fifty years.[24]

Scholars disagree on the meaning and usefulness of the term *mercantilism*. But there is no question that the Atlantic marketplace was shaped by the wish of European maritime empires to restrict foreign ships and goods from full access to their markets. Their reasons were partly economic and partly military. Shipping services generated income, but early modern navies also depended on being able to recruit skilled seamen from merchant ships in wartime, and a large merchant fleet underpinned naval power. Military concerns also dictated the need for maritime empires to be self-sufficient in essential naval stores, such as hemp, tar, and timber for masts and ship construction.

After the Peace of Paris, American trade faced an altered political landscape. Britain offered generous terms for American exports to the British Isles because it was in its best economic interest. However, Britain was much more restrictive about American trade with the West Indies, traditionally an important American export market. In 1783, Britain banned American ships from trading with its Caribbean possessions and also prohibited the importation of many American products that Britain hoped to secure from Canada and the Maritime Provinces of British North America. Meanwhile, the non-British markets that were expected to welcome American custom failed to materialize. In 1784, France prohibited the importation of US flour and wheat to the French West Indies and the exportation of sugar from the islands to North America. France also tried to corner the trade in fish from the Newfoundland fishing banks to the French West Indies, an action of particular concern to New England. Spain was not more forthcoming. Rather than opening markets, it closed the Mississippi River to American boats and goods, thereby imperiling the economic prospects of settlements in the continental interior. Although commercial agreements were signed with minor powers such as Prussia and Sweden, the major trading nations showed scant interest in commercial negotiations with the United States. With no new trading routes or trading partners, the American states remained stuck within the economic orbit of the British Empire but on terms considerably worse than in the colonial period. In 1783, the British politician Lord Sheffield brought this view home in his *Observations on the Commerce of the American States*, in which he argued that as long as disagreements between the states persisted, "it will not be an easy matter to bring the American states to act as a nation." Hence, he concluded, "they are not to be feared as such by us."[25]

The United States could improve its position only by punitive countermeasures. By 1783, members of Congress had realized that Britain and former allies France and Spain were intent on preventing the United States from acquiring a position of power in North America. Late in the year a committee proposed that ships from nations without a commercial treaty with the United States be banned from American ports. Foreign merchants operating in American ports would be allowed to import goods directly from their home countries only if their government had signed a trade agreement with Congress. But such restrictions required amendment of the Articles of Confederation, which in turn required the unanimous support of all thirteen member states. Such support was not forthcoming in either 1783 or 1785, when a more radical proposal was made. As Lord Sheffield had implied, in the eyes of Europe's empires, the American union seemed anything but a formidable enemy in a trade war.

In the Mediterranean trade, American ships suffered from raids by the North African Barbary States. Nominally part of the Ottoman Empire but in reality autonomous, these principalities had long claimed sovereignty over, and the right to intercept ships on, Mediterranean waters. European trading nations therefore paid tribute to Algiers, Tunis, and Tripoli to secure safe passage in the Mediterranean Sea. Cast out of the protection of the British Crown and lacking the funds to arrange treaty payments, US-flagged ships were fair game, and their cargoes and crew were often taken and held for ransom in North Africa. The spectacle of white Christians enslaved by African Muslims troubled Americans and was well publicized in early American plays and novels, such as Susanna Rowson's *Slaves in Algiers* (1794) and Royall Tyler's *The Algerine Captive* (1797). To Americans it seemed that European maritime empires were only too pleased to see American commercial activity in the Mediterranean stall. In a frequently quoted report, Benjamin Franklin claimed to have overheard a London merchant remark, "*If there were no Algiers it would be worth Englands* [sic] *while to build one.*"[26]

The economic prospects of the United States also hinged on developments in the trans-Appalachian West. The peace treaty had awarded the vast territory between the Appalachian Mountains, the Mississippi River, and the Great Lakes to the United States. With rich soils and plentiful natural resources, the Ohio and Mississippi river valleys were universally held to be a region of great potential. Jedidiah Morse, for example, wrote in his *Geography Made Easy* that the Ohio River valley was "the most healthy, the most pleasant, the most commodious and most fertile spot on earth, known to the Anglo Americans." In an age when the economy was still overwhelmingly agricultural, the fertility and abundance of land there meant that the North American interior was destined to become the heartland of a populous and powerful nation.[27]

Yet, unleashing the West's potential was not easy. In a gradual process completed by 1784, the states ceded their colonial claims to land north of the Ohio River to Congress, creating a 260,000-square-mile public domain. By surveying and selling this land to settlers, Congress hoped to reduce the substantial public debt run up during the War of Independence.

But surveying took longer than expected, and the yield from sales was disappointing. Furthermore, payment was made mostly in domestic debt certificates rather than the gold and silver Congress needed to meet the demands of foreign creditors. No matter how much money the western lands might one day be worth, western land sales were not the solution to the union's immediate financial woes.

The problem was primarily geopolitical. The rapid population growth in the early nineteenth century demonstrates that the region was highly attractive to migrants. But in the early 1780s, the Ohio Country was a perilous land. Although Congress's land and government ordinances that laid out the future of the West portrayed it as an empty space, no one was unaware that the region was inhabited and ruled by strong Native American nations. Between 1784 and 1786, Congress negotiated treaties with the Iroquois Confederacy, or Six Nations, the nations of the Northwest Confederacy (the Wyandot, Delaware, Chippewa, Ottawa, and others), and the Shawnee to acquire territory for European American settlers north and west of the Ohio River. But these nations soon had second thoughts and became determined to prevent white settlers from crossing the river.

The indigenous nations' position was bolstered by the continued presence of British traders and army posts south of the Great Lakes. The Native American economy revolved around the exchange of pelts for textiles, tools, small arms, and gunpowder. As long as the native nations could be supplied by the British, they would be able to mount effective resistance to white settler expansion. Adding insult to injury, the posts that the British maintained in the region were located well inside US territory and should have been evacuated in accordance with the treaty of Paris. In order to open up the Ohio Country for settlement, American traders and army garrisons had to replace the British. But the US Army was in no state to mount an attack against the British forts, and in any event the political will to do so was lacking. The diplomatic road was also closed. Several states had breached the 1783 peace treaty by refusing to allow British creditors to sue for debts in American courts. Britain had no cause to surrender its forts before the United States granted British merchants their treaty rights. But under the Articles of Confederation, Congress did not have the means to prevent state legislatures or state courts from violating international agreements.

Spain, too, prevented western expansion. Its long-term aim was to stop the Americans from establishing positions on the Gulf Coast from which they could threaten Spain's transportation routes to Mexico, its principal American possession. Due to North America's topography, its rivers generally flow from north to south, or, less commonly, vice versa, rather than from west to east. The limitations of eighteenth-century communications technology made riverine navigation the most viable means of transportation. Because the majority of rivers empty into the Mississippi, most transports from the interior had to pass New Orleans. Had Americans been subsistence farmers this would hardly have mattered. But in fact almost all farmers in the early United States produced at least in part for the market, and southern planters did so primarily. To complicate matters, many farmers and most planters produced not for the domestic market but for foreign markets. The colonization of the Ohio and Mississippi river valleys by the United States therefore depended on providing settlers with access to national and international markets by allowing them to ship produce downriver to New Orleans. Spain's closure of the Mississippi River to American traffic in 1784 was a fundamental blow to American prospects in the region. Westerners made clear to political leaders on the Atlantic seaboard that, come what may, the river had to stay open. If Congress could not deliver this, settlers were better off as subjects under the Spanish Crown.

In addition to its inability to assert American interests in the Atlantic marketplace and the continental interior, Congress also faced a critical financial situation. The War of Independence had been fought primarily on borrowed money, and in 1783 both the states and the union were heavily indebted to soldiers, contractors, and foreign allies. Under the Articles of Confederation, Congress was expected to requisition money from the states, which were under obligation to meet congressional demands. The system never worked, and its failure became a principal reason for the confederation's downfall. Congress made six requisitions between 1781 and 1786 that together generated an income of slightly more than $5 million. A substantial figure, it was still no more than a third of the sum requested. To make matters worse, the returns on every requisition declined. By the summer of 1786, the financial situation was critical. Congress struggled to avoid default on its Dutch loans and stopped payments on its French and Spanish loans. It could pay neither its small army nor its handful of civil servants.

Several states tried to meet the demands of the union. In the middle years of the 1780s, taxes were three to four times higher than prewar levels, and many states, at least on paper, enforced harsh collection measures. Without ready money and faced with the threat of losing their property through foreclosure, the people protested. Their protests soon paid off when state after state abolished or postponed taxes and provided relief legislation that stayed court proceedings and issued paper currency. Relief measures preserved or restored the social peace but had negative consequences for

Congress. When creditors lost faith in the union they demanded that their home states step in to guarantee their investments, and many state governments answered the call. Out-of-state and foreign creditors had no such option, which led to tensions between states and between the union and other nations. Congress could pay its creditors in Amsterdam only by taking up a new loan to cover interest payments on the old. It was not a sustainable policy, and the credit of the United States plummeted.

The risk of sovereign default had important implications for the ability of the United States to hold its own against other powers. Just as nations do today, eighteenth-century states financed wars and emergencies with borrowed money. As Alexander Hamilton pointed out, "[i]n the modern system of war, nations the most wealthy are obliged to have recourse to large loans," and public credit was therefore of "immense importance" to "the strength and security of nations." But to borrow, a state had to have sufficient income to service its debts. Unless the system of state requisitions was reformed, Congress's credit was unlikely to recover. There was real danger that the young United States would be left to the mercy of stronger nations.[28]

When Congress failed to address the challenges facing American merchants, fishermen, sailors, settlers, land speculators, and creditors, the states stepped into the breach. In doing so, they undermined the case for union. Sometimes their actions also went against the interests of sister states, which further weakened the ligaments of union. Georgia made war on and entered into treaties with the Creek nation; Virginia went to war against the Wabash in the Ohio Country; and Virginia and Maryland concluded a commercial agreement. Some states adopted commercial legislation that discriminated against not only foreign nationals but also out-of-state citizens. Emissions of paper money and adoption of legal-tender laws (which forced creditors to accept paper money as payment for debt) were other sources of interstate and international irritation because they unilaterally altered contracts with foreigners and citizens of other states. State assumption of United States debt obligations made the value of government securities depend not on Congress's credit but on the creditor's domicile, because not all states could afford to assume US debt, and those that could serviced only the debt held by their own citizens.

On the occasions when Congress did act, the consequences were not always positive. The negotiations led by John Jay and Diego de Gardoqui between the United States and Spain over trade and the Mississippi caused the states to fall out along sectional lines. Northern states valued Atlantic commerce more than the Mississippi River trade and were ready to give up the latter for advantages in the former. Southern states, in contrast, were the main source of western migration at the time, and they demanded that the Mississippi River stay open to secure continued migration. In the end, sectional conflict brought the negotiations to a standstill. The Jay-Gardoqui negotiations represent the last attempt of the Confederation Congress to address any of the major challenges facing the new nation. Their failure put an end to Congress's role as an effective decision-making body already by August 1786, almost a year before the Constitutional Convention met.

Although historians have disagreed in their assessments of the 1780s, it is evident that the War of Independence was followed by a severe economic depression. It is also evident that in the postwar period the American union consistently proved itself incapable of performing its basic function to defend and promote the independence and interests of the American states. As a consequence, the language of crisis and despondency was everywhere in the newspapers and pamphlets of the period. The reform-minded Alexander Hamilton summed up the sentiment of despair well when he wrote that the United States had "reached almost the last stage of national humiliation. There is scarcely any thing that can wound the pride, or degrade the character of an independent nation, which we do not experience."[29]

IV. THE MOVEMENT FOR REFORM

D emands for changes in the Articles of Confederation began even before Maryland, as the last state to do so, ratified the agreement in 1781. They would continue right up to 1787, and the Constitutional Convention was but the last in a series of reform attempts. Invariably, these attempts focused on four issues. The first concerned the organization of the federal union and called for a coercive mechanism to secure state compliance with congressional demands. The second concerned the need to create and organize the national domain in the trans-Appalachian West. The two remaining issues concerned the needs to invest Congress with the power to regulate commerce and the power to collect taxes independently of the states. Increased fiscal powers of Congress and the coercion of recalcitrant state governments were closely related questions, because the most serious and persistent state delinquency was the failure of state governments to comply with Congress's requisitions for money. With the exception of the management of the national domain in the West, there was little progress, however. Amendments addressing the other three issues faltered because sectionalism prevented either sufficient support in Congress or the unanimous state approval of amendments demanded by the Articles of Confederation.

In the summer of 1783, two months before the signing of the peace treaty between the United States and Britain, a British order in council closed the British West Indies to American ships. In response, Congress began to consider amending the Articles of Confederation to give Congress the power to regulate commerce. It seemed that strong countermeasures alone could give the United States "reciprocal advantages in trade." Inaction, in contrast, would lead to American commerce slowly expiring in the face of commercial discrimination by rival powers. But effective countermeasures required the coordination of thirteen disparate state policies into one common navigation act. An amendment giving Congress the power to prohibit foreign ships and merchants from trading in American ports was therefore adopted and sent to the states in the spring of 1784. It was never ratified, however. The demand for the centralization of the power to regulate commerce was repeated in 1785 and 1786 in a more sweeping proposal to invest "[t]he United States in Congress Assembled" with the power "of Regulating the trade of the States as well with foreign Nations as with each other and of laying such prohibitions, and such Imposts and duties upon imports, and exports, as may be Necessary for the purpose." On neither occasion did the proposal secure sufficient support in Congress.[30]

In contrast to commercial discrimination, which became an issue only after peace was secured, the problems of the union's empty treasury and of state failure to meet congressional demands had already begun in the midst of the War of Independence. Contemporary critics had no difficulty discerning that the shortage of money arose from a structural flaw in the design of the American confederation. Although the Articles of Confederation invested enough powers in Congress "to answer the ends of our union," there was "no method of enforcing [Congress's] resolutions," the lexicographer and political commentator Noah Webster wrote in the mid-1780s. In other words, the problem was not that the formal powers of Congress were insufficient but that the union was organized in a manner that prevented Congress from exercising them. According to Article VIII, "All charges of war, and all other expences that shall be incurred for the common defence or general welfare, and allowed by the united states in congress assembled, shall be defrayed out of a common treasury." The same article also stated that the "taxes for paying that proportion shall be laid and levied by the authority and direction of the legislatures of the several states within the time agreed upon by the united states in congress assembled." There was therefore no question that the states were constitutionally bound to honor the requisitions and resolutions of Congress. Yet they did not. Critics of the Articles of Confederation believed that the crux of the matter was the absence of a mechanism by which Congress could force states to comply with congressional demands. The articles provided Congress with no sanction or means of coercion to employ against recalcitrant state governments. Instead, the union rested on voluntary compliance. But the "idea of governing thirteen states and uniting their interests by mere *resolves* and *recommendations*, without any penalty annexed to a non-compliance," Webster remarked, in no uncertain terms, "is a ridiculous farce, a burlesque on government, and a reproach to America."[31]

The inadequacies of the union were readily apparent to critics both within and without Congress. In one of the most comprehensive treatises on the problem of union from the early 1780s, the Philadelphia merchant and political economist Pelatiah Webster laid down as his "first and great principle": "That the constitution must vest powers in every department sufficient to secure and make effectual the ends of it."

The supreme authority must have the power of making war and peace—of appointing armies and navies—of appointing officers both civil and military—of making contracts—of emitting, coining, and borrowing money—of regulating trade and making treaties with foreign powers—of establishing post-offices—and in short of doing every thing which the well-being of the commonwealth may require, and which is not compatible to any particular state, all of which require money, and can't possibly be made effectual without it, they must therefore of necessity be invested with a power of taxation.

To ensure compliance with Congress's resolutions, Webster suggested, Congress should have the right to summon and convict any individual who in either a private or a public capacity disobeyed its authority. Should a state government resist by force any act or order of Congress, it would "be lawful for Congress to send into such state a sufficient force to suppress it."[32]

As Pelatiah Webster's pamphlet suggested, the coercive mechanism needed to make states comply with congressional resolutions might have to take severe form. To address this issue, Congress appointed a three-man committee, which included James Madison. The committee report dated March 1781 pulled no punches when suggesting

that in case any one or more of the Confederated States shall refuse or neglect to abide by the determinations of the United States in Congress assembled or to observe all the Articles of the Confederation as required in the 13th. Article, the said United States in Congress assembled are fully authorised to employ the force of the United States as well by sea as by land to compel such State or States to fulfill their federal engagements, and particularly to make distraint on any of the effects Vessels and Merchandizes of such State or States or of any of the Citizens thereof wherever found, and to prohibit and prevent their trade and intercourse as well with any other of the United States and the Citizens thereof, as with any foreign State, and as well by land as by sea, untill full compensation or compliance be obtained with respect to all Requisitions made by the United States in Congress assembled in pursuance of the Articles of Confederation.[33]

It was an extreme proposal that laid bare the inherent flaw of the requisitions system. Expropriating the property of individual citizens to compensate for the delinquencies of their governments was an exceptionally heavy-handed way of administering the nation's finances. It is hardly surprising that the proposal went nowhere. Nor is it surprising that later proposals to invest Congress with coercive power over the states took much milder forms.

The need to replenish the confederation's treasury was the principal reason for amending the Articles of Confederation with the insertion of a coercive mechanism. An alternative means to the same end was to bypass the states and the requisitions system altogether. If Congress were given the right to levy and collect taxes directly from the citizens, the finances of the union could operate without the assistance of the states. This would be the method later favored by the Constitutional Convention in 1787. The ground for the convention's decision had been well prepared by a series of amendment proposals presented in Congress in the years leading up to the Philadelphia Convention.

In 1781, a committee charged with the preparation of "a plan for arranging the finances, paying the debts and economizing the revenue of the United States" advised that Congress be given the right to levy a 5 percent import duty and a 5 percent duty on lawful prizes captured by American privateers. The committee tied taxation directly to the nation's debt obligation by stating that "the monies arising from the said duties be appropriated to the discharge of the principal & interest of the debts already contracted or which may be contracted on the faith of the United States for supporting the present war." Eventually all states except Rhode Island ratified the amendment. Rhode Island remained adamant, and in December 1782, Virginia killed the proposal by rescinding its earlier ratification. The following spring another committee, which included both Hamilton and Madison, repeated the impost proposal as part of a more extensive tax package that also asked the states to contribute $1.5 million annually to Congress. Again the money would be reserved for payment of the union's debt. To make the proposal more palatable to the state governments, this grant of power would run for only twenty-five years. The $1.5 million contribution proved unpopular, but this time both Rhode Island and Virginia accepted the proposal. The amendment now fell instead on New York's refusal to deliver up its lucrative customs income.[34]

After repeated failures to amend the articles, the reform initiative finally passed from Congress to the states. In 1785, Virginia negotiated an agreement with Maryland over the navigation of Chesapeake Bay, and in the following year Virginia invited all states to meet in convention in Annapolis to consider the national regulation of commerce. Only five states sent delegates. No New England state was represented, and apart from Virginia there was no state from the South. Because of poor attendance the convention adjourned almost immediately. But the delegates did at least write a report that spoke of "important defects in the system of the Foederal Government" and of "national circumstances" serious enough "to render the situation of the United States delicate and critical." The Annapolis convention also recommended the calling of a second convention "to devise such further provisions as shall appear to them necessary to render the constitution of the Foederal Government adequate to the exigencies of the Union."[35]

The meeting in Annapolis has traditionally been seen as the prelude to the Philadelphia Convention. But recent research has demonstrated that as late as September 1786, there was little appetite for sweeping reforms of the union in the larger states. In Congress, some delegates argued that the appointment of a constitutional convention undermined Congress's status as the representative assembly of the states and would be the death of the existing confederation. But 1786 saw the woes of the confederation deepen. Lack of revenue meant that default on the foreign debt was imminent and that Congress could protect neither American merchants from Barbary pirates nor frontier families from attacks by Native Americans. Already in February, a congressional committee on the revenue had reported that a "crisis" faced the confederation that would determine the future of the American union. In May, Americans learned that Britain had yet again refused to vacate posts in the Northwest Territory, thereby encouraging Native Americans to step up their raids across the Ohio River. Meanwhile, the impasse in treaty negotiations with Spain further stoked the discontent of western settlers and encouraged talk of secession. As Congress proved unable to address any of the challenges facing the states individually and collectively, the rhetoric of crisis dominated. Yet Congress grew only weaker. Attendance plummeted in 1786, and Congress struggled even to find a quorum.[36]

The sense of escalating crisis made leading reform opponents discontinue or tone down their opposition to a constitutional convention. In November 1786, Virginia authorized the election of delegates to the Philadelphia meeting. New Jersey, Pennsylvania, North Carolina, Delaware, and Georgia followed in the next few months. On February 21, 1787, Congress agreed to call a convention. Nevertheless, skeptics limited its mandate to "revising the Articles of Confederation," thereby hoping to safeguard the continuation of the existing confederation. States accepted the need for reform for different reasons and had different and sometimes conflicting hopes about the outcome. To Virginia, the need for revenue and forceful action on the frontier were paramount. In Massachusetts, the protests against taxation and debt litigation that erupted in Shays's Rebellion united a previously divided political class behind the need for a stronger national government. Reformers in Massachusetts also hoped that a revamped Congress would be able to pursue effective commercial policies. In contrast, their allies in Virginia worried that this would increase the cost of shipping to the detriment of planters. Virginia politicians' wish to strengthen Congress's fiscal powers was not popular in New York, where the government was funded by the productive state impost. A shared sense of crisis and support for reform therefore did not mean that the delegates who gathered in Philadelphia in May 1787 shared the same analysis of the dysfunctions of the union or agreed on how to fix them. Rather, their individual trajectories to the Constitutional Convention were shaped by experiences in their respective states and sections. These varied experiences would guide the convention's deliberations and ultimately shape its outcome.[37]

V. Reforming the Union

No delegate prepared more diligently for the Constitutional Convention than James Madison, who therefore remains the natural starting point for any discussion of its work. In the months leading up to the convention, Madison wrote two memoranda about the political evils that plagued the United States. These texts are rightfully famous, but the most striking fact about them is rarely mentioned: Madison prepared for the convention not by investigating democracies or republics, or even constitutions, but by examining confederations. His "Notes on Ancient and Modern Confederacies" were not concerned with domestic politics or the excesses of democracy as much as with the international and internal relations of past and present unions. He commented extensively on the failure of such confederations to effectively withstand foreign powers and maintain peace and concord among member states. When he turned to an enumeration of the "Vices of the Political System of the United States" in his second memorandum, this focus remained. Only four out of twelve vices referred to the internal affairs of the states. The list instead began with the failure of the states to comply with congressional requisitions. It continued with state encroachments on federal authority; violations of treaties and the law of nations; encroachments by the states on one another's rights; disagreement over commercial regulations and fiscal measures; and the failure to protect the member states from domestic unrest.[38]

Madison outlined his recipe for remedies in a series of letters to fellow Virginia politicians. He concluded that the organizational structure of the federal union, which made Congress dependent on the voluntary compliance of the states, was the fundamental problem facing the American confederation. In this he was far from alone. But Madison had thought further and harder than others about how to fix the problem. Commentators such as Noah Webster and Pelatiah Webster saw the need for a coercive mechanism in the union but had only begun to grasp the need for a separate federal administrative structure. Madison, in contrast, had come to see that the federal government had to be designed so that it could "operate without the intervention of the states." The key to an efficient national government was to keep the states out of the administration of government at the national level and allow Congress to legislate directly on individuals. The national government also needed administrative agencies and a court structure to implement its decisions. Such a drastic change in the operation of government required that the equal representation of states in Congress be replaced by the proportional representation of the citizens. If the federal government would act independently of the states and directly on individuals, the people rather than the states should elect the new government. Finally, to counteract state legislation threatening the common good of the union, the federal government had to have the power to veto state laws. All of these points made their way into the so-called Virginia Plan, which opened and set the agenda for the Constitutional Convention.

Whereas Madison devoted much effort to detailing the reorganization of the union, he was reticent about the specific powers that his new national government would wield. In a letter to Jefferson, written after the convention had adjourned, he claimed that the Constitution aimed not to correct the internal legislation of the states but to secure "the objects of the Union." Unfortunately, he did not reveal what these objects were but spoke merely of the convention's intent "to draw a line of demarcation which would give to the General Government every power requisite for general purposes, and leave to the States every power which might be most beneficially administered by them." A pre-convention letter to George Washington shed only a little more light on this matter. Here Madison noted that the national government would possess all the "federal powers" of the old, together with "positive and compleat authority in all cases which require uniformity, such as the regulation of trade, including the right to tax both exports & imports, the fixing the term and forms of naturalization &c. &c." In the convention, some of Madison's interventions implied that he wished to see a national government with the power to interfere in the domestic affairs of the states. But if this was indeed his wish it was not widely shared among other delegates. Consequently, Madison's later assertion in *The Federalist*, that "if the new Constitution be examined with accuracy and candour, it will be found that the change which it proposes, consists much less in the addition of *new powers* to the Union, than in the invigoration of its *original powers*," remains perhaps the best characterization of the achievements of the Constitutional Convention, if not of his own aspirations.[39]

In all, fifty-five delegates from twelve states attended the Constitutional Convention. Rhode Island alone declined to send any representatives. The delegates were political leaders in their home states, and many of them had served in Congress or held a commission in the Continental army. A majority were lawyers, and almost half were college educated. If they were not quite the assembly of demigods they have sometimes been made out be, and even if some luminaries were absent—John Adams, Patrick Henry, Thomas

Jefferson, and Richard Henry Lee among them—they were undoubtedly a group of men highly qualified to address the problems of the American union. Their discussions were kept frank and open, thanks to the decision to meet behind closed doors, making sure that no details of the convention's debates and its sometimes controversial propositions reached the public.

The convention did not reach a quorum until May 25, 1787, a week after the designated start, and the delay allowed the Virginia delegation to prepare a set of opening resolutions that came to set the agenda for the convention. The acceptance of these resolutions on May 30 signaled the delegates' readiness to supersede their mandate to merely revise the Articles of Confederation and instead establish a national government with a separate legislature, judiciary, and executive. The Virginia resolutions opened by stating that the "articles of Confederation ought to be so corrected & enlarged as to accomplish the objects proposed by their institution; namely, 'common defence, security of liberty and general welfare.'" In his accompanying speech, Virginia delegate Edmund Randolph expanded on this recommendation. He spoke of the "defects of the confederation," pointing to the familiar financial and commercial difficulties that had plagued the American union over the preceding decade. The most pressing matters confronting the confederation were the "inefficiency" of requisitions, "commercial discord" between the states, the urgency of the foreign debt, the violation of international treaties, and the recent tax revolt in Massachusetts associated with Daniel Shays. To address them it was necessary to set up a national government, Randolph asserted, that was able to "secure 1. against foreign invasion: 2. against dissentions between the members of the Union, or seditions in particular states: 3. to p[ro]cure to the several States various blessings, of which an isolated situation was i[n]capable: 4. to be able to defend itself against incroachment: & 5. to be paramount to the state constitutions." Although the third item has an expansive ring to it, Randolph had quite specific blessings in mind, such as "a productive impost," "counteraction of the commercial regulations of other nations," and the ability to increase American commerce "ad libitum."[40]

The Virginia Plan generated strong resistance from the small-state delegates in the convention, but the propriety of the basic remit of the national government outlined by Randolph was not questioned. Connecticut delegate Roger Sherman, who was an outspoken critic of the Virginia resolutions, acknowledged that "the Confederation had not given sufficient power to Congs. and that additional powers were necessary; particularly that of raising money," which, he said, "would involve many other powers." A few days later Sherman defined "[t]he objects of the Union," in a manner quite similar to Randolph, as "1. defence agst. foreign danger. 2. agst. internal disputes & a resort to force. 3. Treaties with foreign nations 4 regulating foreign commerce, & drawing revenue from it." It was these and "perhaps a few lesser objects alone" that "rendered a Confederation of the States necessary." The New Jersey Plan, which was developed as the small states' counterproposal to the Virginia resolutions, also focused on commerce and revenue as the critical issues that had to be addressed by the convention. Like the Virginia Plan, it stipulated that the national legislature would possess "the powers vested in the U. States in Congress, by the present existing articles of Confederation." In addition to these inherited powers, it would also be given the right to levy import duties and a stamp tax and the right to regulate commerce with foreign powers and between the members of the union.[41]

The Philadelphia Convention saw only one early attempt to explicitly enumerate the proper powers of the national government. Introduced by Charles Pinckney of South Carolina, the Pinckney Plan was largely ignored by the other delegates but later came to be used by the Committee of Detail in its draft constitution. By way of this draft, much of Pinckney's enumeration of powers would eventually make its way into the finished Constitution. The South Carolinian's proposal further demonstrates how the convention worked with a rather conventional conception of the proper distribution of powers between the states and the national government along the internal-external distinction. The Pinckney Plan repeated the battery of powers already wielded by Congress under the Articles of Confederation but added the right to levy taxes, including duties on exports and imports, and the right to regulate interstate and international trade.[42]

During the first half of the convention, delegates battled over the principle of representation and postponed debate on the exact powers of the national government. The Virginia Plan had stipulated that the new "National Legislature" be elected by the people rather than the states and that the allocation of seats "ought to be proportioned to the Quotas of contribution [i.e., taxes], or to the number of free inhabitants." This was in marked contrast to the rule under the Articles of Confederation giving all the states an equal vote. Opposition to the Virginia Plan arose from the delegations of New York, New Jersey, Delaware, and Maryland, which at critical points were joined by Connecticut. During the convention these delegations were called "small-state" members, a name that has stuck, despite the fact that some of them represented states that did not differ much in size from some of the so-called large states.[43]

The alternative "small-state" plan, or New Jersey Plan, presented by William Paterson of New Jersey on June 15, left the principle of representation in Congress untouched. Had the plan been accepted, Congress would have continued to be an assembly appointed by and representing the states, and each state would have continued to have one vote in the national council. When the convention rejected the New Jersey Plan on June 19, the small-state members fell back on their second line of defense: demand for state appointment to, and state equality in, one of the two branches of the legislature. They secured this goal in the so-called Connecticut Compromise, which was reached on July 16. The compromise was an important watershed that came approximately halfway into the convention's work. Large- and small-state delegates had clashed violently over the question of representation, and the convention had nearly fallen apart over the issue. Although the agreement reached in mid-July left Madison and other leading delegates disappointed, it allowed the convention to move forward. The Connecticut Compromise was also important in another respect. In the revised plan of union, the states would continue to be directly represented in the Senate, where each of the states would have an equal number of votes. In the House, Madison's vision would prevail: the states would have votes proportional to their populations.

Less well known than the Connecticut Compromise is the equally important solution to Congress's near-total inability to enforce its policies. The Virginia Plan offered no fewer than three institutional solutions to this problem. The first was the creation of a separate national government that could act directly on the people without assistance of the states. By simply leaving the states out of the implementation of the union's decisions, there would be no need to compel them to act. For this reason the Virginia Plan called for a national government that could both make and enforce the law. This government had to possess executive and judicial branches, because a government "without a proper Executive & Judiciary," Virginia delegate George Mason said, in a telling metaphor, "would be the mere trunk of a body without arms or legs to act or move." The proposal to establish a national government capable of acting independently of the states ran headlong into the problem of representation. How could the national government be constructed so that the states would trust it with power to operate beyond their control? After the large and the small states had worked out an agreement in the Connecticut Compromise, the North and the South would clash over the same issue later in the convention. Nevertheless, the creation of a national government that could act directly on the people was the mechanism that would eventually be adopted by the convention to overcome the problem of state delinquency.[44]

The Virginia delegation's other two proposals fared less well, even though they did not raise the problem of representation. The sixth resolution proposed to invest the national legislature with the right "to negative all

laws passed by the several States, contravening . . . the articles of Union."
In Madison's mind this veto power would shield the union from selfish and
shortsighted state legislation. Without it, "every positive power that can be
given on paper" to the national government "will be evaded & defeated"
by the states. "The States will continue to invade the national jurisdiction,
to violate treaties and the law of nations & to harass each other with rival
and spiteful measures dictated by mistaken views of interest." The negative
proposed by the Virginia Plan was actually a diluted version of Madison's
original call for "a negative in *all cases whatsoever*," which his fellow Virginians
presumably found too great an interference with states' rights. Madison's
later attempts to introduce this broader power were also unsuccessful.
Although the convention at first accepted the resolution, this milder veto
was eventually also rejected. Delegates believed that the negative would be
both unpopular and impractical. "Are all laws whatever to be brought up"
to the national legislature? Mason asked on one occasion. "Is no road nor
bridge to be established without the Sanction of the General Legislature? Is
this to sit constantly in order to receive & revise the State laws?"[45]

The convention delegates could reject the idea of the veto because they
had begun to flesh out their concept of parallel structures of state and
national governments. If the national government could act without the
involvement of the state governments, the problem of their inaction, such
as the noncompliance with congressional requisitions, would disappear.
Positive state actions contrary to the interest of the union would remain
a problem, however. Had the convention aimed to set up a national
government to actively regulate the internal affairs of the states, this
would have been a real concern, as the states and Congress would have
found themselves acting and possibly competing in the same sphere of
government activity. But Madison was one of the few delegates who had
such an expansive government in mind. The majority of the delegates did
not, and they preferred to trust to the judiciary to invalidate unconstitutional state laws. "A law that ought to be negatived will be set aside in the
Judiciary departmt.," Pennsylvania delegate Gouverneur Morris said, "and
if that security should fail; may be repealed by a Nationl. law." Sherman
added that the veto involved "a wrong principle, to wit, that a law of a State
contrary to the articles of the Union, would if not negatived, be valid &
operative."[46]

In the finished Constitution, the problem of unconstitutional state
legislation was solved by the "supremacy clause" (Article VI), according to
which the Constitution itself and all laws and treaties made under it became
"the supreme Law of the Land," which "the Judges in every State" were
bound to uphold. The right to appeal from state courts to the Supreme

Court was implicit in Article III of the Constitution and made explicit in the 1789 Judiciary Act. The convention also wrote into the Constitution prohibitions against certain state laws that had appeared especially troubling to the delegates, including those allowing for the printing of paper money and other measures that tended to undermine contractual obligations. With such safeguards in place, and much to Madison's chagrin, the convention felt no qualms about quashing the veto on state laws.

The third and final mechanism for making states adhere to congressional resolutions was military force. According to the Virginia Plan, the new national legislature would have the right "to call forth the force of the Union agst. any member of the Union failing to fulfill its duty under the articles thereof." It was not a new idea. The amendment proposal Madison had helped write in 1781 and the recommendations Pelatiah Webster had published in 1783 asked for the same thing. No sooner had the Virginia delegation presented its resolutions than its members began to have second thoughts, however. They came to realize that a separate national government acting directly on individual citizens would not need the assistance of the states and hence would have no need to coerce them. The very next day, after Randolph had read the resolutions, Mason observed that "punishment could not [in the nature of things be executed on] the States collectively, and therefore that such a Govt. was necessary as could directly operate on individuals, and would punish those only whose guilt required it." Madison had reached the same conclusion. The "more he reflected on the use of force," he said, "the more he doubted the practicability, the justice and the efficacy of it when applied to people collectively and not individually." Using force against a member state "would look more like a declaration of war, than an infliction of punishment, and would probably be considered by the party attacked as a dissolution of all previous compacts by which it might be bound." Although the finished Constitution did give Congress the right to call out the militia "to execute the Laws of the Union," the convention's deliberations made clear that the new national government would not rest on such draconian means to administer its laws.[47]

Coercion was closely linked to revenue because it was the breakdown of the requisitions system that had provided much of the impetus for constitutional reform. The New Jersey Plan put the spotlight on this problem by stipulating that beyond import duties and a stamp tax, the national government would have to continue to resort to requisitions to raise money. Paterson and the other draftsmen of the plan were well aware of the problem with requisitions and provided for the right of the national government to collect taxes in states that failed to comply with them. But the supporters of the Virginia Plan were not impressed. They had now embraced the concept of separate governments and had no patience with requisitions or state involvement in the national revenue system. "There are but two modes, by which the end of a Genl. Govt. can be attained," Randolph remarked. The first was coercion of states; the second was legislation for individuals. "Coercion he pronounced to be *impracticable, expensive, cruel to individuals. . . .* We must resort therefore to a national *Legislation over individuals.*" Mason questioned the practicality of the New Jersey Plan. "Will the militia march from one State to another, in order to collect the arrears of taxes from the delinquent members of the Republic?" he asked. As Madison had done, Mason also pointed out that such a "mixture of civil liberty and military execution" was incompatible with a republican system of government resting on the consent of the governed. "To punish the non-payment of taxes with death, was a severity not yet adopted by despotism itself: yet this unexampled cruelty would be mercy compared to a military collection of revenue, in which the bayonet could make no discrimination between the innocent and the guilty."[48]

VI. SECTIONALISM AND THE RENEWED COMPACT OF STATES

During the months of June and July, the convention had gradually come to an agreement on the questions of state representation and the organization of the new government. States would be represented in the Senate, state populations in the House of Representatives. There would be a tripartite national government capable of acting independently of the states and directly on individuals. But beyond general statements that the national government would inherit all "the Legislative Rights vested in Congress by the Confederation," along with an undefined grant "to legislate in all cases to which the separate States are incompetent, or in which the harmony of the United States may be interrupted by the exercise of individual Legislation," which had been made in the Virginia resolutions, there had been no sustained discussion about what the new government was expected to do, and what it would not be allowed to do. This would change when the convention received the Committee of Detail's draft constitution on August 6 and had to confront the question about the extent of the powers to be invested in the new national government. In the course of the debate that followed over the next few weeks, sectional interests came to the fore in discussions that revolved primarily around questions of Congress's power to tax and regulate commerce. These were deeply entwined issues, because commercial regulation often took the form of prohibitive taxes on imports and exports rather than outright bans on foreign ships and goods. The undisguised sectionalism evident in these discussions cast doubt on the existence of any shared sense of a larger national interest that could serve to balance the strong sectional concerns of the delegates.[49]

The convention had already come close to falling apart over the fear that large states would oppress small states. That debate produced some of the less edifying moments of the deliberations. Paterson at one point declared that New Jersey would rather "submit to a monarch, to a despot" than be governed by a coalition of large states. Gunning Bedford Jr. of Delaware threatened that, unless the large states accepted equal representation of states in the Senate, the small states would "find some foreign ally of more honor and good faith, who will take them by the hand and do them justice." Outbursts like these led other delegates to question the idea that size determined state interests in any meaningful sense, however. The real conflict of interest in the United States, Alexander Hamilton said, was between "carrying & non-carrying States, which divide instead of uniting the largest States." "Carrying," in the language of the eighteenth century, referred to the shipping interest. Reluctantly, Madison, too, conceded the existence of conflicting interests in the union. They stemmed not from size, however, but from "climate" and "principally from [the effects of] their having or not having slaves."[50]

The convention debates thereafter came to be dominated by a conflict of interest not between small and large states but between the interests identified by Hamilton and Madison as running between the slave states of the South and the carrying states of the North that were dependent on international trade. During this debate, delegates were anything but coy in promoting the interests of their own states. In a typical intervention, Gouverneur Morris demanded guarantees for the "maritime" interests against free-trade legislation sponsored by southern states. South Carolina delegate Pierce Butler, meanwhile, explained that the "security the Southn. States want is that their negroes may not be taken from them which some gentlemen within or without doors, have a very good mind to do." This perception of fundamental sectional incompatibility as well as the confrontational style of debate came to shape the outcome of the Constitution in important ways.[51]

Although it was composed of three Northerners and two Southerners, the Committee of Detail responsible for the first full draft of the Constitution had nevertheless assimilated southern fears that a northern-dominated Congress would betray the South's particular commercial interests. The committee's report thus proscribed Congress from taxing exports and from taxing, or otherwise interfering with, the slave trade. It also stipulated that Congress could pass commercial legislation only with the support of two-thirds of the members of both houses.[52]

As a bloc of staple-producing states, the South had an interest in free trade and cheap transportation. It was "the true interest of the S. States to have no regulation of commerce," noted South Carolina delegate Charles Cotesworth Pinckney at one point. Northern and middle states, in contrast, had extensive shipping interests that were threatened by international competition. Shipping was "the worst & most precarious kind of property and stood in need of public patronage," Northerners argued. Such patronage would most likely take the form of navigation acts of the kind Britain had imposed on its colonies. These would raise shipping costs by forcing staple producers to ship their goods in American-flagged vessels. This inherent conflict of interest between North and South was usually defused by pointing to a sectional trade-off. The South and its slave economy could be safe from external attack and slave insurrection only with support from the North, especially from its naval strength. "A navy was essential to security, particularly to the S. States, and can only be had by a navigation act encouraging american bottoms [i.e. ships] & seamen," said Morris. It was a sign of the sectional tensions appearing in the convention that some southern delegates now denied the existence of this trade-off. "It had been said that the Southern States had the most need of naval protection," Maryland's John Francis Mercer observed. "The reverse was the case. Were it not for promoting the carrying trade of the Northn States, the Southn States could let their trade go into foreign bottoms, where it would not need our protection." Hugh Williamson of North Carolina feared no foreign invasion of the South, as "[t]he sickliness of their climate for invaders would prevent their being made an object."[53]

During the debate over the Committee of Detail's report, delegates from the middle states tried to roll back some of the South's gains. They were only partially successful. The taxing of exports seemed to these delegates both proper and necessary. Morris argued that a tax on the export of lumber, livestock, and flour would put pressure on Britain to open the West Indies to American trade because the islands could not survive without such imports. It was also "a necessary source of revenue." A coalition of Southerners and New Englanders refused to budge, however. Because the "produce of different States is such as to prevent uniformity in such taxes," a duty on exports would be unjust and would therefore "engender incurable jealousies." The proscription against national export taxes was upheld by a vote of seven states to three, with only the small states of New Hampshire, New Jersey, and Delaware opposed to the measure.[54]

Luther Martin of Maryland next proposed to do away with the ban on interference with the slave trade. As could be expected, this was not well received by the delegations from the lower South, whose constituents were dependent on the importation of enslaved Africans. The preservation of the slave trade was declared the sine qua non for the Carolinas and Georgia. Charles Pinckney made it clear that "South Carolina can never receive the plan if it prohibits the slave trade." After an animated discussion, Morris moved that the clause on the slave trade and the ban on export taxes be referred to a committee along with the demand for a two-thirds majority for all navigation acts. "These things may form a bargain among the Northern & Southern States," he suggested. Just before the vote on Morris's motion was taken, Massachusetts's Nathaniel Gorham reminded the southern delegates that "the Eastern States had no motive to Union but a commercial one. They were able to protect themselves. They were not afraid of external danger, and did not need the aid of the Southn. States."[55]

Morris was right that an intersectional bargain could be found. Within two days the committee came back with a watered-down version of the Committee of Detail's stipulations. Congress would be permitted to legislate on the slave trade after the year 1800 and would be allowed to tax the importation of enslaved persons. Struck out was the section stating: "No navigation act shall be passed without the assent of two-thirds of the members present in each House." The ban on export duties was left to stand. In the ensuing debate the protection of the slave trade was extended to 1808, and the import duty on slaves set to a maximum of ten dollars per imported enslaved person. Some southern delegates made an effort to retain the qualified majority necessary to pass commercial legislation, but by now their compatriots were in a mellow mood. Charles Cotesworth Pinckney pointed to the Northerners' "liberal conduct" on the slave question as sufficient cause to leave "the power of making commercial regulations" unfettered. Northern delegates meanwhile stressed that they could not agree to the Constitution unless they were "enabled to defend themselves against foreign regulations." Nathaniel Gorham asked, "If the Government is to be so fettered as to be unable to relieve the Eastern States what motive can they have to join in it, and thereby tie their own hands from measures which they could otherwise take for themselves?" The decision to strike out the demand for a qualified majority was accepted without objection.[56]

The South had thus successfully blocked the right of the national government to tax exports. They were also successful in defending their interests by shaping the rules of representation in the House of Representatives. The Virginia Plan had suggested that representation be calculated either according to "the Quotas of contribution" or to "the number of free inhabitants." The former was a reference to the manner of apportioning expenditures between the states under the Articles of Confederation. In 1783, Congress had accepted a committee proposal that contributions no longer be based on state wealth, which had been stipulated in the articles, but on population. Under the new system, contributions would be "in proportion to the whole number of white and other free citizens and inhabitants, of every age, sex and condition, including those bound to servitude for a term of years, and three fifths of all other persons not comprehended in the foregoing description, except Indians, not paying taxes, in each state." In the convention, Southerners and Northerners disagreed on whether or not to include enslaved persons when calculating state populations for purposes of representation. After a long and tortuous process, in which the delegates tried to accommodate southern interests without making use of the objectionable term *slavery*, the convention finally adopted the three-fifths rule for apportioning both representatives in the lower House and direct taxes. The South was also successful in securing a fugitive-slave clause, which stipulated that escaped slaves could be apprehended and returned to slavery anywhere in the United States, and tacit agreement on the principle that the national government should keep its hands off the internal police of the states, including the matter of slavery's legality. By means of the three-fifths clause, the fugitive-slave clause, the guarantee for the continuation of the international slave trade to 1808, and the proscription against national government interference with slavery in the states, the Constitution safeguarded the future of slavery in the United States.[57]

The debate on the powers of the national government drew attention to the fact that the exercise of federal powers, for example over trade and taxation, would produce different economic consequences in different states. Convention delegates demonstrated a readiness to compromise, up to a point, but their readiness did not extend to core sectional interests. As the debate over representation had shown, delegates were even less prone to compromise on the question of their state's corporate identity. In principle, the convention could have written the Constitution as a blueprint for a consolidated nation-state, providing for the dissolution of the existing states and the reconfiguration of the political geography of the United States. After all, the states had a recent and in many cases contingent history. During the debate on the Virginia Plan's provision for proportional representation, Nathaniel Gorham pointed out that Massachusetts was an amalgamation of three earlier colonies, and Connecticut and New Jersey of two. The opposite process had also appeared in the history of Britain's North American settlements. North and South Carolina had once been one colony, as had Pennsylvania and Delaware. At one point in the debate, Paterson had suggested that "all State distinctions must be abolished, the whole must be thrown into a hotchpot, and when an equal division is made, then there may be fairly an equality of representation." Another delegate wished "that a map of the US be spread out, that all the existing boundaries be erased, and that a new partition of the whole be made into 13 equal parts." But such proposals were hardly serious. Not even the so-called nationalists in the convention showed any interest in dissolving the existing states. To the contrary, Madison and other delegates held that representation had to be proportional to population precisely because the large states were anxious to retain their ability to defend and promote their particular interests and would not accept the bid to empower the national government unless they could also influence its actions.[58]

Contingent history or not, by 1787 all states, large and small, had become reified entities in the American political imagination. Citizens owed their primary allegiance to the state governments and supported the union as the means to protect the independence and interests of their states. No wonder therefore that the delegates to the Philadelphia Convention did not act like a "band of brothers" but like political negotiators looking out for the best interests of their constituents. Delegates worked from the assumption that the states were different and that their interests were in potential conflict. "Each State like each individual had its peculiar habits usages and manners, which constitutes its happiness," Roger Sherman explained. And no state would "give to others a power over its happiness, any more than an individual would do, if he could avoid it." Had there not been a strong sense that the United States consisted not just of thirteen polities but of thirteen polities with distinct interests, there would have been no bickering over the distribution of votes between the states and the sections. And there would have been no need for the three-fifths compromise that gave the southern states votes on the basis of both their free and enslaved populations.[59]

An important, if sometimes overlooked outcome of the Constitutional Convention was therefore the reconfirmation of the states as the principal political organization in the American federal union. The union was designed to preserve the states, not to replace them. Rather than a competitor to the states, the new national government was their creation and a powerful tool to realize interests they were too weak to effect on their own. The intellectual home to a powerful anti-statist ideology, the South would nonetheless benefit greatly from using the federal government to protect slavery, remove the Native American population, acquire land for cotton plantations, and promote American exports. But Northerners benefited, too, from government land policies that ensured that just like the planters of the South they could reproduce their societies across the North American continent.

VII. Ratification of the Constitution

The Constitutional Convention adjourned on September 17, 1787, and in a dramatic gesture, three of the delegates—Elbridge Gerry of Massachusetts, George Mason, and Edmund Randolph—refused to put their signatures to the finished Constitution. For Gerry and Mason the chief reason was fear that the convention had gone too far in creating a strong central government and had failed to safeguard basic civic rights and liberties. Their objections foreshadowed a widespread critique that would be directed against the Constitution when it became known to the people out of doors.

When the members of the convention approved of the Virginia resolutions, they also approved a ratification process, whereby their plan for a more perfect union would be accepted or rejected not by Congress or the states but by special conventions appointed by popular election, meaning the votes of free adult males. The Constitution was therefore forwarded to Congress with the recommendation that "it should afterwards be submitted to a Convention of Delegates, chosen in each State by the People thereof, under the Recommendation of its Legislature, for their Assent and Ratification." As Article VII of the Constitution made clear, ratification by nine states was required for it to take effect. Critics in Congress objected, claiming that the Constitutional Convention had exceeded its mandate and that the Articles of Confederation prevented Congress from approving the Constitution. Richard Henry Lee echoed the concerns of Gerry and Mason by proposing amendments for the protection of civic rights. But the majority favored immediate action and quickly agreed to submit the Constitution to the states with the request that they call ratifying conventions. Several of the states also acted with dispatch. Five states called conventions within a month. By the end of the year, five more had followed. South Carolina called its convention in January, and New York did so on February 1, 1788. Only Rhode Island chose to ignore the recommendation of Congress.[60]

The first of the ratifying conventions to assemble was Pennsylvania's, on November 20, 1787. North Carolina's, which began on July 21, 1788, was the last. From the perspective of the Federalists, the ratification process got off to a good start. Between December 7, 1787, and January 9, 1788, five states ratified the Constitution with little or no opposition. Only in Pennsylvania did the anti-Federalists put up a determined fight. But their critique proved resilient, taking on life as the contest moved to other states. Thus, the objection that the Constitution lacked a bill of rights to ensure against the overreach of the new federal government and the demand that it be amended by a second constitutional convention came to resonate widely beyond Pennsylvania. Nonetheless, the Federalist majority in Pennsylvania held sway, and the state was among the first to ratify the new Constitution. Only with the Massachusetts convention did the march toward ratification begin to slow. Opposition to the Constitution was strong there, and compromise was required to secure adoption. Moderate Federalists proposed that the Constitution be adopted together with a series of amendments that would strengthen the rights of individuals and limit the federal government's powers over the states. This proposal won over enough anti-Federalists to allow the ratification of the Constitution by a close vote of 187 to 168 on February 6, 1788. Ratification with recommended amendments would henceforth become the Federalists' strategy for placating the opposition, and with the exception of Maryland, every state that ratified the Constitution after Massachusetts also proposed amendments. The narrow vote in Massachusetts was followed by a setback in New Hampshire, where the Federalists escaped defeat only by accepting a four-month adjournment. Maryland, in April 1788, and South Carolina, in May, proved to be solidly Federalist, however, and in June 1788, New Hampshire became the ninth state to ratify the Constitution, thereby establishing the new government.

Without ratification by New York and Virginia, the future of the American union was nevertheless still in doubt. In Virginia, Federalists and anti-Federalists were equally strong, whereas New York was overwhelmingly anti-Federalist. Both states came to ratification by narrow margins, Virginia by ten votes in June 1788, and New York by only three a month later. In both states the vote was influenced by the timing of the ratifying convention. Because they met relatively late in the process, after the nine ratifying votes were essentially secured, the convention delegates found themselves with a stark choice: to ratify the Constitution or leave the union. Under these circumstances ratification seemed the less bad choice. With New York and Virginia in favor, it mattered little that North Carolina and Rhode Island at first rejected the Constitution. Eventually, both states called new conventions and ratified in 1789 and 1790, respectively. Three years after the adjournment of the Philadelphia Convention, all of the thirteen original states had accepted the new compact.

Within a few weeks after the adjournment of the Constitutional Convention, sixty-one of the eighty American newspapers then in operation had printed the Constitution in full, and the plan was also published as pamphlets and broadsides. The press frequently reported on the debates in the ratification conventions, and the newspapers were also filled with essays and letters discussing the pros and cons of ratification. Even by twenty-first-century standards, the scope of the ratification debate is impressive. The modern critical edition of the public and private debates thus far published, the *Documentary History of the Ratification of the Constitution*, amounts to fifteen thousand pages of print, collected in twenty-seven volumes—and several additional volumes are projected. The supporters of the Constitution, who had adopted the name "Federalists," controlled most of the newspapers and dominated the debate. Yet the voice of the opposition was distinctly heard, both in print and at ratifying conventions. Because of the bare-bones nature of the records from the Constitutional Convention, scholars have turned to this debate to elucidate the meaning of the Constitution and the aspirations of its supporters.

Federalists had branded the critics of the Constitution "anti-Federalists," thus suggesting that they advocated disunion or smaller regional confederations. It mattered little that the vast majority of anti-Federalist writers and politicians not only supported the American union but accepted the need for the Articles of Confederation to be reformed. Their real concern was that the Constitution had gone too far in creating a government with unlimited power to raise armies and taxes, regulate the militia, borrow money, and pass any law "deemed necessary and proper." The new federal government, anti-Federalists feared, would be invested with such boundless legislative and judicial power that it would inevitably "annihilate the state governments, and swallow them up in the grand vortex of general empire." This notion that the Constitution aimed at the "consolidation" of the thirteen American republics into "one entire government" became a staple of anti-Federalist rhetoric. One opponent of the Constitution asked "whether the thirteen United States should be reduced to one great republic, governed by one legislature, and under the direction of one executive and judicial [*sic*]; or whether they should continue thirteen confederated republics, under the direction and controul of a supreme federal head for certain defined purposes only."[61]

Contemporary political theory defined democratic republics as states governed by popular consent to the law and popular participation in the administration of the law. As a result, theorists supposed, there were strict limits on a republic's geographic and demographic size. Once the ratio of legislators to electors became too low, electors would lose trust in their representatives and legislators would lose their knowledge of the needs and mores of their constituents. The consequence would be legislation poorly suited to the wishes of the people and of doubtful legitimacy. Such laws

would not be administered by the people voluntarily but would either
be ineffective or put in effect by government officers empowered to act
without regard for the popular will. To the anti-Federalists, the national
government proposed by the Constitution simply seemed incompatible
with republican rule. By creating a strong president eligible for reelection,
a small House of Representatives with a ratio of only one representative
for every thirty thousand inhabitants, and a small Senate with a six-year
term, the convention had set up a government that would be unresponsive
to the wishes of the common people and beyond the effective control of
the citizens. As a result, it was destined to fall under the control of the rich
and well born who would use the new government to oppress the people
and to increase their own riches and prestige. Anti-Federalists found further
evidence of such class bias in the Constitution's proscriptions against paper
money and debt relief, and its protection of the sanctity of contracts.
Although the federal government might perhaps be able to act with energy
against foreign nations, this ability would come at the price of a centralization of power that would eventually put an end to popular liberty.

The anti-Federalists hoped to maintain a political union in which state
sovereignty was less circumscribed and in which states and sections had
a better chance to prevent the national government from acting in ways
detrimental to their essential interests. To this effect they proposed a
number of structural amendments to safeguard the sovereignty of the states
and restrict the powers of the national government. In contrast to the early
proposals by Mason and Lee, the anti-Federalist amendments at their core
did not aim to protect the civic rights of individuals as much as the corporate
identity and rights of the states. They asked that federal officers take an
oath not to violate the rights of the states; that the federal government be
proscribed from interfering with state public finance, state taxation, or
state militia regulations; and that no commercial treaty be approved that
infringed on the powers and rights of the states. They wanted a two-term
limit on the presidency, limits on the scope of federal court jurisdiction,
and restrictions on Congress. The limits on Congress included a demand
for a qualified majority to raise an army in peacetime and to enter into
commercial agreements with foreign powers. Anti-Federalists also wished
to prevent Congress from levying direct taxes or excises and from creating
merchant monopolies.

The Federalists never accepted their opponents' analysis of the
Constitution. They argued that the federal government rested on the
principle of popular representation and that it would exercise its powers for
the benefit of the people. They also refused to compromise on the specific
clauses of the Constitution to which their opponents objected. To them,

the far-ranging fiscal powers and the supremacy and general welfare clauses, as well as other powers invested in the federal government, were necessary if the new government were to perform its duties. However, the Federalists tried hard to assuage their opponents' fear that the states would be absorbed by the national government, by insisting that they, too, subscribed to the idea of a union in which two levels of government coexisted and divided up the task of governing roughly along the internal-external divide that had also been the hallmark of the Articles of Confederation. They presented the national government as a government of limited and enumerated powers and accepted that duties not explicitly delegated to Congress were retained by the states. According to Pelatiah Webster, "the new Constitution leaves all the Thirteen States, complete republics, as it found them, but all confederated under the direction and controul of a federal head, for certain defined national purposes only, i.e. it leaves all the dignities, authorities, and internal police of each State in free, full, and perfect condition; unless when national purposes make the controul of them by the federal head, or authority, necessary to the general benefit."[62]

The main theme in Federalist rhetoric was the contrast between the blessings of union and the horrors of disunion. No friends of the Constitution used it to better effect than Alexander Hamilton, John Jay, and James Madison, the authors of *The Federalist*, a work that remains the most famous exposition of the Constitution. *The Federalist* presented the American people with the choice not between alternative ways to reform the union but between the Constitution and disunion. According to *The Federalist*, disunion would result in the creation of mutually antagonistic regional confederacies, which would build up their military strength and enter into alliances with Europe's great powers. War was bound to follow, and in its wake the political centralization and decline of liberty that anti-Federalists feared. Wars gave rise to standing armies, heavy taxes, and large public debts, a trinity of evil that Madison once described as the bane of republics and the maker of monarchies. Adoption of the Constitution, in contrast, promised to secure the future of the union and thereby to banish war from the North American continent.[63]

The Federalist also urged the critics of the Constitution to accept that the American republic existed in a world of predatory monarchies. If the self-rule of the American people in their respective states was to be maintained, their national government had to be able to defend the independence and interests of the United States. Ultimately, this defense rested on the ability to project military power, which required that unlimited authority over mobilization be granted to the federal government. If left to themselves, the states could mobilize sufficient resources to defend their interests only by exerting a heavy pressure on their citizens. In contrast, by joining forces, they could establish enough strength to ward off hostile powers with a minimum imposition on the people. Thus, the Constitution promised the benefits of government at a nearly negligible cost.

The ratification debate is perhaps most famous for being the genesis of the Bill of Rights, the first ten amendments to the Constitution. It is often said that the Bill of Rights was the anti-Federalists' lasting contribution to the Constitution and that its adoption was instrumental in turning erstwhile critics of the Constitution into reluctant supporters. Yet this reading is colored by the importance that the Bill of Rights took on in the twentieth century and ignores the contemporary reaction to the amendments from anti-Federalists. The Bill of Rights was shepherded through Congress not by anti-Federalists but by a Federalist, James Madison. The few anti-Federalists in the Senate and House of Representatives consistently opposed Madison and derided his amendment proposals as a deception, calling them "a tub to the whale." This curious expression referred to the practice of sailors of the time, when troubled by a whale, to throw out a barrel, or "tub," to divert the creature's attention away from their ship.[64]

Madison surely understood what his critics were after. He admitted in private that his amendments were designed to have minimal effect on "the structure and stamina" of the federal government. During the ratification struggle, anti-Federalists proposed roughly one hundred changes to the Constitution. Two-thirds of these aimed at the structure of the union and aimed to retain power and sovereignty in the states. Madison virtually ignored these, and Congress included only three structural amendments in the proposal they sent to the states. Instead, Madison concentrated on procedural amendments to protect individual civic rights. Anti-Federalists had proposed around thirty of these, and Madison incorporated three-quarters of them into his draft Bill of Rights. In time these rights would become immensely important in American political life, but they did not address the principal anti-Federalist objections to the Constitution. Senator William Grayson of Virginia, one of the few anti-Federalists in the first Congress, remarked that "[s]ome gentlemen here from motives of policy have it in contemplation to effect amendments which shall effect [sic] personal liberty alone, leaving the great points of the Judiciary, direct taxation, &c. to stand as they are." Once the people's fears of unlimited government had been put to rest by a phony set of inconsequential amendments, the Federalists would "go on cooly [sic] sapping the independence of the state legislatures."[65]

In the very long run, the anti-Federalists' dire warning that the Constitution created the conditions for a federal government with authority and power to make the states conform to national standards in their social, economic, and civic life did come true. By exempting the federal government from constitutional constraints when dealing with external affairs, such as war, international trade, and immigration, and by the strategy of "surrogacy," whereby creative interpretation allowed enumerated powers to be stretched "to achieve unenumerated policy goals," the president, the Congress, and the Supreme Court made the federal government all-encompassing. Yet this was largely a twentieth-century development, and it certainly did not spring ready-made from the Constitutional Convention. To the contrary, the framers of the Constitution envisaged the American union as a means to protect and promote the corporate identity and interests of the member states, not to destroy and replace them. And they expected that under the Constitution the states would continue to order their internal affairs in accordance to the wishes of their citizens, as they had done under both British imperial rule and under the Articles of Confederation.[66]

CONCLUSION:
A NEW APPROACH TO THE
CONSTITUTIONAL SETTLEMENT OF 1787

The internationalist interpretation of the founding presented here puts the spotlight on foreign and intra-union affairs as the genesis of the Constitution, whereas the economic interpretations of progressive scholars have focused on domestic matters. But this shift in perspective does not mean that economic interpretations have become redundant. To the contrary, the internationalist interpretation's focus on the question of home rule makes possible a fresh look at the core progressive concern with who should rule at home. By presenting the Constitution as a federal treaty that left the internal arrangement of the states largely alone, the internationalist perspective forces us to recognize that the ground rules determining who should rule at home were created through a much more complex process, taking place at different levels of government and involving multiple sources of law, than the progressive account allows. And by highlighting the role of the federal government in commercial and territorial expansion, it opens new areas that can be fruitfully analyzed as sites of struggle between social groups over material resources. A proper understanding of the constitutional settlement of 1787 requires us to recognize the impact of the Constitution and the Northwest Ordinance on the organization of the western borderlands and the impact of the Constitution on international relations in the Atlantic marketplace. But it also means going beyond the Constitution and national politics to account for change and stasis at state and local levels.

In 1787, the trans-Appalachian West made up roughly half the national domain of the United States. To exclude this enormous region and its population from the analysis of who came to rule at home is surely impossible after Native American and borderlands historians have emphasized their importance to the course of American history for decades. In fact, their work asks other historians to recognize that what is at stake in the struggle over who should rule at home is not only the distribution of political authority but also the geographic boundaries of what the United States claimed as its "home." The fiscal, military, and administrative resources that the Constitution invested in the new federal government made possible the gradual transformation of the West into American republics. In the train of federal soldiers came surveyors and land agents, followed by settler colonists. Between 1791 and 1810, treaties with Native American nations transferred some 170,000 square miles of land—an area almost two and a half times the size of New England—to the United States, the bulk of which was passed on to white settlers. They filled up the land quickly. In 1790, there were 110,000 settler colonists living in what became the states of Kentucky and Tennessee. By the turn of the eighteenth century, that figure had almost tripled. An additional 50,000 settlers resided in territories that would become Ohio and Indiana. Of the Kentucky residents in 1800, some 40,000 were enslaved people forcefully removed from the Chesapeake, thus highlighting how western expansion was also slavery's expansion. This peopling of the West was made possible only by the removal of the Native American proprietors of the land and the disciplining of the ethnically and culturally mixed borderlands population that chose to remain.[67]

In the short term, the Constitution's effect on Atlantic trade was overshadowed by the impact of the long European and global war triggered by the French Revolution. But throughout the 1790s and the early nineteenth century, American trade expanded dramatically and brought riches to Atlantic port cities, thanks at least in part to the now internationally recognized "treaty worthiness" of the United States. This successful and prolonged immersion in the Atlantic marketplace ensured that the southern states would continue to be major exporters of agricultural staple products such as tobacco, rice, indigo, sugar, and, above all, cotton. The expansion of these staples, due to their mode of production, also caused the expansion of slavery. In 1790, close to seven hundred thousand persons, almost one in five inhabitants, were enslaved in the United States. In 1861, the enslaved numbered four million. They too have to be part of our account of who came to rule at home.[68]

The removal and decimation of Native Americans and the demographic and geographic expansion of slavery point to the need to look beyond the overt political struggles of white males when analyzing the distribution of power and social resources that resulted from the constitutional settlement of 1787. The "social death" of the slave represents an extreme case of total negation of rights to property and person. Others too had their rights and liberty circumscribed. In fact, the vast majority of early American inhabitants lived under the authority of a master who possessed far-reaching rights to their bodies, labor, and property. So-called household government formed the bedrock of the American republics. Social and legal historians have shown how under its laws wives were subject to their husbands, children to their father, and servants to their master. Household government cannot be dismissed as a marginal phenomenon, because for most people it was the only government they knew. As Carole Shammas has pointed out, "[m]ost inhabitants of early America had no direct access to the state; the household head mediated between his dependents, whether children, wife, servants, slaves, or wards, and formal government bodies." The question of who, in the most literal sense, was to rule at home is central to any story of the American founding that aims at inclusiveness.[69]

The Constitution is silent on the law of the household for the simple reason that it remained a matter of state regulation after 1787. Rather than radical reform, the citizens of the newly independent American states and their elected leaders chose to perpetuate and accentuate a socio-legal order put in place during colonial times. Continuity rather than change characterized household government in the age of revolution. As Shammas puts it: "Considering the amount of constituting writing that went on, what is most remarkable is the reluctance to rein in the powers of the household head." This was due to neither oversight nor lethargy. To the contrary, a core element of republican citizenship was the power of the citizen over his dependents. Household government was complemented by local government institutions—town meetings, county courts, slave patrols—which stepped in when masters failed to maintain or control their household dependents, and which coordinated and administered tasks that individual households could not undertake on their own, such as poverty relief, road construction, and adjudication. Like the rights and duties of citizens and their dependents, these institutions were created and regulated by state rather than federal law. William Novak has shown that far from a laissez-faire society, in which government intervention in social and economic affairs was shunned, a "distinctive and powerful governmental tradition devoted in theory and practice to the vision of a well-regulated society dominated United States social and economic policy-making" in the nineteenth century. Whereas Novak tends to embrace this tradition of "police regulation" as the expression of local self-determination, Gary Gerstle and others have highlighted how the citizenry's command over local governmental institutions was used for the surveillance, punishment, and reform of those who fell outside the control of the patriarchal household—single women, the destitute, non-"whites," vagrants, and aliens.[70]

If the Constitution was a federal treaty, investigations of the struggle over who should rule at home, in all its complexity, need to pay attention to the federal government but also to look carefully at what was happening in state assemblies and town meetings. But such investigations cannot stop there. They have to go beyond even the politics of the street to investigate power structures and power struggles in the allegedly apolitical spaces of the courtroom, the workplace, the congregation, the orphanage, the asylum, and the household and the family.

FURTHER READING

No survey or interpretation, however extensive or well written, can convey the richness of the primary sources of the founding era. Historians of the US Constitution are exceedingly fortunate in having access to a number of superb documentary histories, many of them freely available on the Internet. Paul H. Smith et al., eds., *Letters of Delegates to Congress, 1774–1789*, 26 vols. (Washington, DC: Library of Congress, 1976–2000); and Worthington C. Ford et al., eds., *Journals of the Continental Congress, 1774–1789*, 34 vols. (Washington, DC: Library of Congress, 1904–37), are essential guides to the activities of the Continental Congress up to 1789. Max Farrand, ed., *The Records of the Federal Convention of 1787*, 4 vols. (New Haven, CT: Yale University Press, 1966 [1937], 2nd ed.), complemented with James J. Hutson, ed., *Supplement to Max Farrand's Records of the Federal Convention of 1787* (New Haven, CT: Yale University Press, 1987), is the source for the Constitutional Convention. Mary Sarah Bilder, *Madison's Hand: Revising the Constitutional Convention* (Cambridge, MA: Harvard University Press, 2015), raises important questions about the integrity of James Madison's notes from the convention, which have always been the principal source to the proceedings; it is now required reading. The *Journals*, the *Letters*, and Farrand's *Records* are all available on the Library of Congress's website *A Century of Lawmaking for a New Nation: U.S. Congressional Documents and Debates, 1774–1875* (https://memory.loc.gov/ammem/amlaw/lawhome.html).

William T. Hutchinson and William M. E. Rachal, eds., *The Papers of James Madison*, 17 vols. (Chicago: University of Chicago Press, 1962–91), should be consulted for the thought of the principal founding father. Volume 9 covers the winter and spring of 1787, when Madison wrote several important letters and memoranda in preparation for the Constitutional Convention. An electronic version of this critical edition, together with the modern critical editions of the papers of five other major statesmen of the period—John Adams, Benjamin Franklin, Alexander Hamilton, Thomas Jefferson, and George Washington—are freely available on the National Archives' website *Founders Online* (http://founders.archives.gov/). The enormous debate over ratification is reproduced in Merrill Jensen, John P. Kaminiski, and Gaspare J. Saladino, eds., *The Documentary History of the*

Ratification of the Constitution, 27 vols. to date (Madison: State Historical Society of Wisconsin, 1976–). It is available electronically on the University of Virginia Press website *Rotunda* (http://www.upress.virginia.edu/rotunda), but access requires a subscription. The first federal Congress has its own documentary history: Linda Grant DePauw et al., eds., *Documentary History of the First Federal Congress of the United States of America, March 4, 1789–March 3, 1791*, 20 vols. (Baltimore, MD: Johns Hopkins University Press, 1972–2012).

Bernard Bailyn, the doyen of early American history, once remarked that other than the Bible, no document had received more commentary than the US Constitution. This interest reflects not only the Constitution's importance in the historical evolution of the United States but also its role in contemporary American politics and law. It is safe to say that no book has exerted greater influence on the field's understanding of the Constitution than Charles A. Beard's *An Economic Interpretation of the Constitution of the United States* (New York: Macmillan, 1913). It remains required reading. Beard presented the Constitution as the outcome of a class struggle between the socioeconomic elite and ordinary farmers and artisans. Modern historians working in the spirit of Beard include Woody Holton, *Unruly Americans and the Origins of the Constitution* (New York: Hill and Wang, 2007); Terry Bouton, *Taming Democracy: "The People," the Founders, and the Troubled Ending of the American Revolution* (New York: Oxford University Press, 2009); Barbara Clark Smith, *The Freedoms We Lost: Consent and Resistance in Revolutionary America* (New York: The New Press, 2010); and Michael J. Klarman, *The Framers' Coup: The Making of the United States Constitution* (New York: Oxford University Press, 2016). Gordon S. Wood, *The Creation of the American Republic, 1776–1787* (Chapel Hill: University of North Carolina Press, 1969), remains the classic study of origins of the Constitution. Like Beard, it highlights class struggle as the central cause of the Constitution, but, in contrast to Beard, its ironic reading claims that despite the intentions of the Federalists the outcome was the democratization of American society.

The interpretation offered in the preceding pages owes more to a group of scholars who see the Constitution not as the response to domestic class struggle but to problems of federalism and international relations. Pioneering this perspective were Jack P. Greene, *Peripheries and Center: Constitutional Development in the Extended Polities of the British Empire and the United States, 1607–1788* (Athens: University of Georgia Press, 1986); and Peter S. Onuf, *The Origins of the Federal Republic: Jurisdictional Controversies in the United States 1775–1787* (Philadelphia: University of Pennsylvania Press, 1983). Later followers include Max M. Edling, *A Revolution in Favor of*

Government: Origins of the U.S. Constitution and the Making of the American State (New York: Oxford University Press, 2003); David C. Hendrickson, *Peace Pact: The Lost World of the America Founding* (Lawrence: University Press of Kansas, 2003); and David M. Golove and Daniel J. Hulsebosch, "A Civilized Nation: The Early American Constitution, the Law of Nations, and the Pursuit of International Recognition," *New York University Law Review* 85, no. 4 (2010): 932–1066.

Succinct and intelligent overviews of the major issues in the scholarly literature are provided by Alan Gibson, *Interpreting the Founding: Guide to the Enduring Debates over the Origins and Foundations of the American Republic* (Lawrence: University Press of Kansas, 2010, 2nd ed.); and Gibson, *Understanding the Founding: The Crucial Questions* (Lawrence: University Press of Kansas, 2010, 2nd ed.). Alfred F. Young and Gregory H. Nobles, *Whose American Revolution Was It? Historians Interpret the Founding* (New York: New York University Press, 2011), is an insightful and sympathetic reading of the progressive interpretation and its successors. Appearing in time for the Constitution's bicentennial, Leonard W. Levy and Dennis J. Mahoney, eds., *The Framing and Ratification of the Constitution* (New York: Macmillan, 1987), has authoritative essays by leading historians on various aspects of the founding that have withstood the test of time.

Merrill Jensen's *The New Nation: A History of the United States during the Confederation, 1781–1789* (New York: Knopf, 1950), emphatically denied the existence of a "critical period" in the 1780s. A modern, careful, and nuanced assessment of the period and the breakdown of the first American union is offered in George W. Van Cleve, *We Have Not a Government: The Articles of Confederation and the Road to the Constitution* (Chicago: University of Chicago Press, 2017). Jack N. Rakove, *The Beginnings of National Politics: An Interpretative History of the Continental Congress* (New York: Knopf, 1979), is essential reading about what was taking place in Congress in this period. Jensen, Rakove, and Van Cleve are also the best guides to the Articles of Confederation, together with another classic work by Merrill Jensen, *The Articles of Confederation: An Interpretation of the Social-Constitutional History of the American Revolution, 1774–1781* (Madison: University of Wisconsin Press, 1940).

Historians have investigated many aspects of the postindependence period. Alan Kulikoff, "'Such Things Ought Not to Be': The American Revolution and the First National Depression," in *The World of the Revolutionary American Republic: Land, Labor, and the Conflict for a Continent*, ed. Andrew Shankman (New York: Routledge, 2014), 134–64; Peter H. Lindert and Jeffrey G. Williamson, "American Incomes Before and After the Revolution," *Journal of Economic History* 73, no. 3 (2013):

/15 65, Lindert and Williamson, *Unequal Gains: American Growth and Inequality since 1700* (Princeton, NJ: Princeton University Press, 2017); and John J. McCusker, "Estimating Early American Gross Domestic Product," *Historical Methods* 33, no. 3 (2000): 155–62, estimate the impact of the War of Independence and postwar commercial restrictions on trade and economic growth. In addition to Golove and Hulsebosch, above, Eliga Gould, *Among the Powers of the Earth: The American Revolution and the Making of a New World Empire* (Cambridge, MA: Harvard University Press, 2012), looks at the problem of international recognition. Leonard J. Sadosky, *Revolutionary Negotiations: Indians, Empires, and Diplomats in the Founding of America* (Charlottesville: University of Virginia Press, 2009), deals with early US diplomacy with European great powers and Native American neighbors as interconnected issues. Important new works on the trans-Appalachian West both before and after the adoption of the Constitution include William H. Bergmann, *The American National State and the Early West* (New York: Cambridge University Press, 2012); Patrick Griffin, *American Leviathan: Empire, Nation, and Revolutionary Frontier* (New York: Hill and Wang, 2007); and Bethel Saler, *The Settlers' Empire: Colonialism and State Formation in America's Old Northwest* (Philadelphia: University of Pennsylvania Press, 2015). For the Northwest Ordinance, see Peter S. Onuf, *Statehood and Union: A History of the Northwest Ordinance* (Bloomington and Indianapolis: Indiana University Press, 1987). Gregory Ablavsky, "The Savage Constitution," *Duke Law Journal* 63, no. 5 (February 2014): 999–1088, makes the case that the Constitution was intended to deal with Native Americans in the West. The troubled finances of the Confederation Congress are analyzed and explained in Roger H. Brown, *Redeeming the Republic: Federalists, Taxation, and the Origins of the Constitution* (Baltimore, MD: Johns Hopkins University Press, 1993); and E. James Ferguson, *The Power of the Purse: A History of American Public Finance, 1776–1790* (Chapel Hill: University of North Carolina Press, 1961).

Narrative accounts of the Constitutional Convention range from the classic work by Max Farrand, *The Framing of the Constitution of the United States* (New Haven, CT: Yale University Press, 1913), and another classic, by Clinton Rossiter, *1787: The Grand Convention* (New York: Macmillan, 1966), to recent works by Carol Berkin, *A Brilliant Solution: Inventing the American Constitution* (New York: Houghton Mifflin Harcourt, 2003), and Richard Beeman, *Plain, Honest Men: The Making of the American Constitution* (New York: Random House, 2009). The best analytical works of the convention are Cathy D. Matson and Peter S. Onuf, *A Union of Interests: Political and Economic Thought in Revolutionary America*

(Lawrence: University Press of Kansas, 1990); Lance Banning, *The Sacred Fire of Liberty: James Madison and the Founding of the Federal Republic* (Ithaca, NY: Cornell University Press, 1995); and Jack N. Rakove, *Original Meanings: Politics and Ideas in the Making of the Constitution* (New York: Knopf, 1996). For Madison's veto proposal, see Charles F. Hobson, "The Negative on State Laws: James Madison, the Constitution, and the Crisis of Republican Government," *William and Mary Quarterly*, 3rd ser., vol. 36, no. 2 (April 1979): 215–35. The significance of slavery in the Constitutional Convention is the subject of George W. Van Cleve, *A Slaveholders' Union: Slavery, Politics, and the Constitution in the Early American Republic* (Chicago: University Press of Chicago, 2010); and David Waldstreicher, *Slavery's Constitution: From Revolution to Ratification* (New York: Hill and Wang, 2009). Howard A. Ohline, "Republicanism and Slavery: Origins of the Three-Fifths Clause in the United States Constitution," *William and Mary Quarterly*, 3rd ser., vol. 28, no. 4 (October 1971): 563–84, was the first study of slavery and representation in the Constitution.

The history of the ratification struggle is masterfully told by Pauline Maier, *Ratification: The People Debate the Constitution 1787–1788* (New York: Simon & Schuster, 2010). Patrick T. Conley and John P. Kaminski, eds., *The Constitution and the States: The Role of the Original Thirteen in the Framing and Adoption of the Federal Constitution* (Madison: University of Wisconsin Press, 1988); and Michael Allen Gillespie and Michael Lienesch, eds., *Ratifying the Constitution* (Lawrence: University Press of Kansas, 1989), are collections of essays on each of the states. On the anti-Federalists, see Herbert J. Storing, *What the Antifederalists Were For: The Political Thought of the Opponents of the Constitution* (Chicago: University of Chicago Press, 1981); and Saul Cornell, *The Other Founders: Anti-Federalism and the Dissenting Tradition in America, 1788–1828* (Chapel Hill: University of North Carolina Press, 1999). A recent study of *The Federalist* is Max M. Edling, "'A Vigorous National Government': Hamilton on Security, War, and Revenue," in *The Cambridge Companion to "The Federalist,"* ed. Jack N. Rakove and Colleen Sheehan (New York: Cambridge University Press, forthcoming). The standard source for the first federal Congress is Kenneth R. Bowling, *Politics in the First Congress, 1789–1791* (New York: Garland, 1990). The fifth chapter is a very important analysis of the Bill of Rights that Bowling published as a separate article: "'A Tub to the Whale': The Founding Fathers and Adoption of the Federal Bill of Rights," *Journal of the Early Republic* 8 (1988): 223–51. Stanley Elkins and Eric McKitrick, *The Age of Federalism: The Early American Republic, 1788–1800* (New York: Oxford University Press, 1993), remains unsurpassed for the politics of the 1790s. Several studies deal with specific issues of the period. Chapters 2 and

3 of Max M. Edling, *A Hercules In the Cradle: War, Money, and the American States, 1783–1867* (Chicago: University of Chicago Press, 2014), treats the reforms of fiscal policy and the public debt; Richard H. Kohn, *Eagle and Sword: The Federalists and the Creation of the Military Establishment in America, 1783–1802* (New York: Free Press, 1975), is still the best work for the military; Gautham Rao, *National Duties: Custom Houses and the Making of the American State* (Chicago: University of Chicago Press, 2016), covers the creation of the important revenue service. Bergmann, Sadosky, and Saler, cited above, should be consulted for developments in the West. Chapters 2 and 3 of William Earl Weeks, *The New Cambridge History of American Foreign Relations*, vol. 1: *Dimensions of the Early American Empire, 1754–1865* (New York: Cambridge University Press, 2013), is a recent and up-to-date overview of the diplomacy of the period.

ENDNOTES

1. "From George Washington to the States, 8 June, 1783," *Founders Online*, National Archives, last modified April 12, 2018 [Early Access document], http://founders.archives.gov/documents/Washington/99-01-02-11404.

2. John Fiske, *The Critical Period of American History, 1783–1789* (Boston: Houghton Mifflin, 1899 [1888]), 55; Gordon S. Wood, *The Creation of the American Republic, 1776–1787* (Chapel Hill: University of North Carolina Press, 1969), 393.

3. "Congressional Ratification of the Definitive Treaty of Peace," in *The Emerging Nation: A Documentary History of the Foreign Relations of the United States under the Articles of Confederation, 1780–1789*, ed. Mary A. Giunta (Washington, DC: National Historical Publications and Records Commission, 1996), 1:963–67.

4. Fiske, *Critical Period*, 223.

5. Ibid., vi–vii.

6. Ibid., 308–9; Charles A. Beard and Mary R. Beard, *The Rise of American Civilization*, 2 vols. (New York: Macmillan, 1955 [1930 rev. ed.]), 1:332–33.

7. Charles A. Beard, *An Economic Interpretation of the Constitution of the United States* (New York: Macmillan, 1913), 48; Beard and Beard, *Rise of American Civilization*, 1:303.

8. Merrill Jensen, *The Articles of Confederation: An Interpretation of the Social-Constitutional History of the American Revolution 1774–1781* (Madison: University of Wisconsin Press, 1976 [1940]), xv and 245; Jensen, *The New Nation: A History of the United States during the Confederation, 1781–1789* (New York: Knopf, 1950), 128, 423.

9. Peter S. Onuf, "A Declaration of Independence for Diplomatic Historians," *Diplomatic History* 22, no. 1 (1998): 71–83; David Armitage, *The Declaration of Independence: A Global History* (Cambridge, MA: Harvard University Press, 2007); Leonard J. Sadosky, *Revolutionary Negotiations: Indians, Empires, and Diplomats in the Founding of America* (Charlottesville: University of Virginia Press, 2009); David M. Golove and Daniel J. Hulsebosch, "A Civilized Nation: The Early American Constitution, the

Law of Nations, and the Pursuit of International Recognition," *New York University Law Review* 85, no. 4 (2010): 932–1066, quotation at 934; Eliga H. Gould, *Among the Powers of the Earth: The American Revolution and the Making of a New World Empire* (Cambridge, MA: Harvard University Press, 2012); Robbie J. Totten, "Security, Two Diplomacies, and the Formation of the U.S. Constitution: Review, Interpretation, and New Directions for the Study of the Early American Period," *Diplomatic History* 36, no. 1 (2012): 77–117.

10. Carl Lotus Becker, *The History of Political Parties in the Province of New York, 1760–1776* (Madison, WI: Bulletin of the University of Wisconsin, no. 286, History series, vol. 2, no. 1, 1909): 5.

11. Michael P. Zuckert, "Federalisms and the Founding," *Review of Politics* 48 (1986): 174.

12. Montesquieu, *The Spirit of the Laws*, ed. Anne M. Cohler, Basia Carolyn Miller, and Harold Samuel Stone (Cambridge: Cambridge University Press, 1989), part 2, book 9, ch. 1, 131–32; Emer de Vattel, *The Law of Nations, Or, Principles of the Law of Nature, Applied to the Conduct and Affairs of Nations and Sovereigns, with Three Early Essays on the Origin and Nature of Natural Law and on Luxury*, ed. Richard Whatmore and Béla Kapossy (Indianapolis: Liberty Fund, 2008), 84.

13. John Locke, *Two Treatises of Government*, ed. Peter Laslett (Cambridge: Cambridge University Press, 1988), 365; Montesquieu, *Spirit of the Laws*, 156–57.

14. James Wilson, "Lectures on Law, Delivered in the College of Philadelphia," in *Collected Works of James Wilson*, ed. Kermit L. Hall and Mark David Hall, 2 vols. (Indianapolis: Liberty Fund, 2007), 1:664; St. George Tucker, *View of the Constitution of the United States, with Selected Writings*, ed. Clyde N. Wilson (Indianapolis: Liberty Fund, 1999), 80; "Committee Report on Carrying the Confederation into Effect and on Additional Powers Needed by Congress," in *Documentary History of the Ratification of the Constitution*, ed. Merrill Jensen, John P. Kaminski, and Gaspare J. Saladino, 27 vols. to date (Madison: Wisconsin Historical Society Press, 1976–), 1:145.

15. Alexander Hamilton, *The Farmer Refuted, &c.*, in *Papers of Alexander Hamilton*, ed. Harold C. Syrett, 27 vols. (New York: Columbia University Press, 1961-1987), 1:81–165, quotation at 98; Thomas Jefferson, "Draft of Instructions to the Virginia Delegates in the Continental Congress (MS Text of *A Summary View*, &c.), [July 1774]," in *The Papers of Thomas Jefferson*, ed. Julian P. Boyd., 40 vols. to date (Princeton, NJ: Princeton University Press, 1950–), 1:121–137; John Adams, "Novanglus VII: To the

Inhabitants of the Colony of Massachusetts-Bay, 6 March 1775," in *Papers of John Adams*, ed. Robert J. Taylor et al., 17 vols. to date (Cambridge, MA: Harvard University Press, 1977–), 2:307–27.

16. John Adams, "Novanglus VII," ibid.

17. Heather Schwartz, "Re-Writing the Empire: Plans for Institutional Reform in British America, 1675–1791" (unpublished PhD dissertation, SUNY Binghamton, 2011), Appendix A, 245–55; Jack N. Rakove, *The Beginnings of National Politics: An Interpretative History of the Continental Congress* (New York: Knopf, 1979), 136–38.

18. For the text of these plans, see Joseph Galloway's "Plan of Union," September 28, 1774, in *Journals of the Continental Congress*, ed. Worthington C. Ford et al., 34 vols. (Washington, DC: Library of Congress, 1904–37), 1:49–51; Franklin's "Articles of Confederation," July 21, 1775, in *Journals of the Continental Congress*, 2:195–99; Silas Deane's proposal to Congress, November 1775 [?], in *Letters of the Delegates to Congress, 1774–1789*, ed. Paul H. Smith et al., 25 vols. (Washington, DC: Library of Congress, 1776–2000), 418–20; Connecticut plan, *Pennsylvania Evening Post*, March 5, 1776.

19. *Journals of the Continental Congress*, 5:425, 428–29, 431, 433.

20. Articles of Confederation and Perpetual Union, in *Documentary History of the Ratification of the Constitution*, 1:86–91.

21. Samuel von Pufendorf, *Of the Law of Nature and of Nations* (London, 1729), book 7, ch. 5, 681–83.

22. The drafts of the Dickinson committee are in *Journals of the Continental Congress*, 5:674–89.

23. For the tension between the states and Congress over Native American diplomacy in the 1780s, see Sadosky, *Revolutionary Negotiations*.

24. John J. McCusker, "Estimating Early American Gross Domestic Product," *Historical Methods* 33, no. 3 (2000): 155–62.

25. John Holroyd, Earl of Sheffield, *Observations on the Commerce of the American States with Europe and the West Indies* (London: J. Debrett, 1783), 68.

26. Benjamin Franklin to Robert R. Livingston, July 22[–26], 1783, in *Papers of Benjamin Franklin*, ed. Ellen R. Cohn et al., vol. 40 (New Haven, CT: Yale University Press, 2011), 369.

27. Jedediah Morse, *Geography Made Easy: Being an Abridgement of the American Geography* (Boston: Isaiah Thomas & Ebenezer T. Andrews, 1790, 2nd ed., abridged by the author), 231.

20. Alexander Hamilton, "Federalist 30," in *The Federalist*, ed. Jacob E. Cooke (Middletown, CT: Wesleyan University Press, 1961), 192; Hamilton, "Defence of the Funding System," in *Papers of Alexander Hamilton*, 19:60.

29. Alexander Hamilton, "Federalist 15," in *Federalist*, 91.

30. "Grant of temporary power to regulate commerce," April 30, 1784, in *Documentary History of the Ratification of the Constitution*, 1:154; "Amendment to grant commercial powers to Congress," March 28, 1785, ibid., 155; "Amendments to the Articles of Confederation proposed by a Grand Committee of Congress," August 7, 1786, ibid., 164.

31. Noah Webster, *Sketches of American Policy* (Hartford, CT: Hudson and Goodwin, 1785), 44.

32. Pelatiah Webster, *A Dissertation on the Political Union and Constitution of the Thirteen United States, of North America* (Philadelphia: T. Bradford, 1783), 6-7, 42.

33. "Amendment to give Congress coercive power over the states and their citizens," in *Documentary History of the Ratification of the Constitution*, 1:142–43.

34. "Grant of power to collect import duties," in *Documentary History of the Ratification of the Constitution*, 1:140–41; "Grant of temporary power to collect import duties and request for supplementary funds," April 18, 1783, ibid., 146–48.

35. "Proceedings and Report of the Commissioners at Annapolis, Maryland," September 11–14, 1786, ibid., 184.

36. George W. Van Cleve, *We Have Not a Government: The Articles of Confederation and the Road to the Constitution* (Chicago: University of Chicago Press, 2017).

37. "Confederation Congress Calls the Constitutional Convention," February 21, 1787, in *Documentary History of the Ratification of the Constitution*, 1:187.

38. James Madison, "Notes on Ancient and Modern Confederacies" and "Vices of the Political System of the United States," in *Papers of James Madison*, ed. William T. Hutchinson and William M. E. Rachal, 17 vols. (Chicago: University of Chicago Press, 1962–91), 9:3–24, 345–58.

39. Madison to Thomas Jefferson, October 24, 1787, in *Papers of James Madison*, 10:207–8; Madison to George Washington, April 16, 1787, ibid., 9:383; James Madison, "The Federalist No. 45," in *Federalist*, 314.

40. "The Virginia Resolutions," in *Documentary History of the Ratification of the Constitution*, 1:243–45; Max Farrand, ed., *The Records of the Federal*

Convention of 1787, 4 vols. (New Haven, CT: Yale University Press, 1966 [1937], 2nd ed.), 1:18–19, 20.

41. Farrand, *Records*, 1:34, 133, 243.

42. Farrand, *Records*, 2:158–59.

43. Farrand, *Records*, 1:20.

44. Farrand, *Records*, 1:124. On the Connecticut Compromise and the convention's debate about representation, see Richard Beeman, *Plain, Honest Men: The Making of the American Constitution* (New York: Random House, 2009), 200–25; and Jack N. Rakove, *Original Meanings: Politics and Ideas in the Making of the Constitution* (New York: Knopf, 1996), 57–70.

45. Farrand, *Records*, 1:21, 164–68, 2:27–28, 390–92; Madison to George Washington, April 16, 1787, in *Papers of James Madison*, 9:383–84.

46. Farrand, *Records*, 2:27–28.

47. Farrand, *Records*, 1:21, 34, 54. In a letter to Thomas Jefferson, Madison remarked that an administration of the laws relying on coercion of delinquent states resembled "much more a civil war, than the administration of a regular Government"; Madison to Thomas Jefferson, October 24, 1787, in *Papers of James Madison*, 10:207.

48. Farrand, *Records*, 1:243, 256, 339–40.

49. Farrand, *Records*, 1:21.

50. Farrand, *Records*, 1:179, 492, 466, 486.

51. Farrand, *Records*, 1:604, 605.

52. Farrand, *Records*, 2:182–83.

53. Farrand, *Records*, 2:307–8, 449, 450.

54. Farrand, *Records*, 2:307, 360, 363–64.

55. Farrand, *Records*, 2:305–8, 359–65, 369–75.

56. Farrand, *Records*, 2:400, 414–17, 449–53.

57. Farrand, *Records*, 1:20; "Amendment to Share Expenses According to Population," April 18, 1783, in *Documentary History of the Ratification of the Constitution*, 1:148–50.

58. Farrand, *Records*, 1:177, 178, 462.

59. Farrand, *Records*, 1:343, 467.

60. "Virginia Resolutions," in *Documentary History of the Ratification of the Constitution*, 1:245; "Resolutions of the Convention Recommending the Procedures for Ratification and for the Establishment of Government under the Constitution of the Confederation Congress, 17 September

1787," ibid., 318, "Proceedings of Congress on the Constitution," ibid., 322–42.

61. "The Dissent of the Minority of the Convention," *Pennsylvania Packet*, December 18, 1787, in *Documentary History of the Ratification of the Constitution*, 2:629; "Letters of the Federal Farmer," ibid., 14:24; "Brutus I," *New York Journal*, October 18, 1787, ibid., 13:413.

62. [Pelatiah Webster], *The Weakness of Brutus Exposed*, in *Documentary History of the Ratification of the Constitution*, 14:71.

63. James Madison, "Political Observations," April 20, 1795, *Papers of James Madison* 15, 558.

64. Kenneth R. Bowling, "'A Tub to the Whale': The Founding Fathers and Adoption of the Federal Bill of Rights," *Journal of the Early Republic* 8 (1988): 223–51.

65. Madison to Edmund Randolph, June 15, 1789, in *Papers of James Madison*, 12:219; Grayson to Patrick Henry, June 12, 1789, quoted in Kenneth R. Bowling, *Politics in the First Congress, 1789–1791* (New York: Garland, 1990), 136.

66. On exemption from constitutional constraints and "surrogacy," see Gary Gerstle, *Liberty and Coercion: The Paradox of American Government from the Founding to the Present* (Princeton, NJ: Princeton University Press, 2015), 89–123, quotation at 93.

67. Charles J. Kappler, ed., *Indian Affairs: Laws and Treaties*, vol. 2 (Treaties) (Washington, DC: Government Printing Office 1904); *Eighteenth Annual Report of the Bureau of American Ethnology to the Secretary of the Smithsonian Institution 1896–97*, pt. 2: *Indian Land Cessions in the United States 1784–1894*, 56th Cong., 1st Sess., H.R. doc. no. 736/3, 56th Cong., 1st Sess. (1899), U.S. serial set no. 4015; *Indians Removed to West Mississippi from 1789*, H.R. doc. 147, 25th Cong., 3rd Sess. (1838), Statement B, 9; U.S. Bureau of the Census, *Historical Statistics of the United States, Colonial Times to 1970*, bicentennial ed., 2 vols. (Washington, DC, 1975), 1:24–37. Peter S. Onuf interprets this process in *Jefferson's Empire: The Language of American Nationhood* (Charlottesville: University Press of Virginia, 2000), 18–52, 147–88; and in "The Empire of Liberty: Land of the Free and Home of the Slave," in *World of the Revolutionary American Republic*, ed. Andrew Shankman (New York: Routledge, 2014), 195–217. See also Bernard W. Sheehan, *Seeds of Extinction: Jeffersonian Philanthropy and the American Indian* (New York, 1974); Peter S. Onuf, *Statehood and Union: A History of the Northwest Ordinance* (Bloomington and Indianapolis: Indiana University Press, 1987); Bernard W. Sheehan, "The Indian Problem in the

Northwest: From Conquest to Philanthropy," in *Launching the "Extended Republic": The Federalist Era*, ed. Ronald Hoffman and Peter J. Albert (Charlottesville: University Press of Virginia, 1996), 190–222; Bethel Saler, *The Settlers' Empire: Colonialism and State Formation in America's Old Northwest* (Philadelphia: University of Pennsylvania Press, 2014).

68. Stanley Elkins and Eric McKitrick, *The Age of Federalism: The Early American Republic, 1788–1800* (New York: Oxford University Press, 1993), 375–449; John Craig Hammond, "The 'High-Road to a Slave Empire': Conflict and the Growth and Expansion of Slavery on the North American Continent," in Shankman, *World of the Revolutionary American Republic*, 559-98. Among the progressives, Staughton Lynd saw this clearly in *Class Conflict, Slavery, and the United States Constitution* (Indianapolis and New York: Bobbs-Merrill, 1967), 135–213.

69. Christopher Tomlins, *Freedom Bound: Law, Labor, and Civic Identity in Colonizing English America, 1580–1865* (Cambridge: Cambridge University Press, 2010), 16–17, 401–508; Stephanie McCurry, *Masters of Small Worlds: Yeoman Households, Gender Relations, and the Political Culture of the Antebellum South Carolina Low Country* (New York: Oxford University Press, 1995); Carole Shammas, *A History of Household Government in America* (Charlottesville: University of Virginia Press, 2002), quotation at xiii; Laura F. Edwards, *The People and Their Peace: Legal Culture and Transformation of Inequality in the Post-Revolutionary South* (Chapel Hill: University of North Carolina Press, 2009); Carole Smith-Rosenberg, *This Violent Empire: The Birth of an American National Identity* (Chapel Hill: University of North Carolina Press, 2010).

70. Jack P. Greene argues for the persistence of the states as the principal polity also after the adoption of the Constitution in "Colonial History and National History: Reflections on a Continuing Problem," *William and Mary Quarterly*, 3d. ser. (2007): lxiv; Shammas, *History of Household Government in America*, 65; William J. Novak, *The People's Welfare: Law and Regulation in Nineteenth-Century America* (Chapel Hill: University of North Carolina Press, 1996), quotation at 1; Gary Gerstle, "The Resilient Power of the States across the Long Nineteenth Century: An Inquiry into a Pattern of American Governance," in *The Unsustainable American State*, ed. Lawrence Jacobs and Desmond King (New York: Oxford University Press, 2009); Gerstle, *Liberty and Coercion*, 59–86.